FIRST TIME
PROPERTY DEVELOPER

A Beginners Guide To Developing
Residential Property For Profit

by Nick Fox

ISBN: 978-0-9935074-5-8

First published in England in 2017 by Fox Print Partners

FIRST TIME PROPERTY DEVELOPER

A Beginners Guide To Developing
Residential Property For Profit

By Nick Fox

published by Fox Print Partners

Contents

For my family, friends and business partners.
You all inspire me daily. Thank you.
Nick

About the author

Nick Fox is an experienced property developer, mentor, author and speaker with a property portfolio worth in excess of £35 million. What is remarkable is that he built this portfolio in less than a decade!

Most people would probably leave it at that sit back and think what a great retirement they will have to look forward to. Nick has other ideas. He is driven to helping others achieve the same levels of success he has enjoyed as a property developer. This book is designed to help other first time property developers learn from the mistakes and successes he has experienced along the way.

Nick's approach to property investment draws upon the wisdom of the world's most successful investors combined with his own experience as a successful entrepreneur.

His first experience of business came early in life at just eight years old in the school tuck shop. Instead of saving up his pocket money, he decided to invest it and make a profit selling penny sweets for the inflated price of 2p each. This may have been small change and seem like child's play, yet buying something for a low price and selling it for a higher price is one of the basic building blocks of any business and that includes property investment.

The return on investment from those tuck shop sweets was 100% and this was an early indication of an entrepreneurial mind-set, which helped Nick grow a technology business from scratch to a multi-million-pound enterprise. He later went on to apply those same basic principles successfully into property investment.

Nick's involvement in property investment was no accident of fate apart from an early introduction in his childhood. He lived in a static home with his mother and everyone was happy with their lot until it burned down and the family was forced to look for alternative accommodation.

Luckily, the insurance money they received for the damage helped them to buy a house, which was a complete wreck. With a bit of hard work this was soon transformed into saleable property and generated enough profit to move onto the next house and so on.

Nick bought his own first property in 1986, at the age of 18 when many young people are still thinking about which University degree to opt for. The property was purchased with the money he had managed to earn and save from his early entrepreneurial market stall trading.

It wasn't until the mid-2000s that Nick decided to jump into property investment full time and before doing so he read every property book and visited every website he could find to gain insight into the world of property from an investor's point of view. Then he soon got stuck in to developing his own portfolio.

Beyond property, Nick is a keen supporter of various charities and a patron of Peace One Day.

He currently lives in London with his partner Samantha, their two sons Harold and Albert and three wonderful daughters Molly, Lily and Masie.

Also by Nick Fox:

HMO Property Success

The Secrets of Buy to Let Success

Property Investment Success

Complete Property Investment Success

HMO Property Renovation & Refurbishment Success

101 Top Tips for Property Investment Success

The HMO Home Study Guide

Available in paperback from nickfox.co.uk & Amazon.co.uk
Audiobook available from Amazon.co.uk and Audible.co.uk
Kindle and iBook formats also available

Author's disclaimer

I am not qualified to give financial or legal advice. All related recommendations made in this book should only be considered in consultation with suitably qualified and accredited professionals. Persons giving financial advice MUST be properly qualified and regulated by the Financial Services Authority (FSA) and anyone giving you legal advice should be suitably qualified and regulated by The Law Society and the Solicitors Regulation Authority (SRA) (or the Council of Licensed Conveyancers (CLC)).

Foreword

Ever heard the story of London's buried diggers?

The story goes that sometime in the recent past, many of London's wealthy property owners decided to extend the space in their homes by digging out their basements.

The value these basements added to the houses and the potential disruption caused by the removal of the diggers meant that it wasn't cost effective to dig them out and they remain buried as a result.

The Telegraph newspaper reported that there could be up to 1,000 JCBs buried in the basements of these London houses and they are doomed to remain there until a time when property in London isn't so valuable.

The story was soon found to be total nonsense, yet it has become something of an urban myth, which even the national newspapers and ITV news bought into at the time. This tells us two things; don't believe everything you read and anything is possible when it comes to property development, even if it isn't yet an option to bury a perfectly good JCB when you're done with the building work.

When I was a youngster I still remember the sense of pride my mum and I had when we turned what was a wreck of a property into something that would eventually sell for tens of thousands of pounds more than it was worth originally.

This taught me a lot about how a bit of hard work had the potential to transform our lives when it was channelled into something we controlled.

It was a simply a twist of fate that we were forced to move out of our static home following a fire. Opportunities often come from setbacks like this and it is the ability to recognise and build on those opportunities that brings success in most things including property.

Property development has been around since people in London lived in timber framed houses. Even before the Great Fire destroyed many of them, rents and property prices were high enough in the city for people to be thinking about building extensions across their back yards and regular refurbishment so that they could make money from tenants.

The population of London at that time was around 80,000, which is a little over a large football stadium full of people! Things have moved on quite a bit since then, but fast forward to today and the fundamental principles remain the same. We have seen London property prices rise to astronomical levels and rents soar.

A trend set to continue across the UK for the foreseeable future.

All of this has a ripple effect on the rest of the country when the economy is performing well. Small pockets of cities and towns across the UK become more expensive places to live and it is in these areas where the opportunities for profiting from property development can be found.

Demand for property in sought after areas means that more of it needs to be built and this is where property developers come in. If you become a property developer, you are helping to satisfy this demand either by building new or developing existing properties to make them more desirable or perhaps turning them into houses of multi occupation (HMOs) or student properties.

Are You a Property Developer or a Property Investor?

Property development and property investment mean different things to different people. In reality the two couldn't be more closely related. You can of course be a property investor without being a developer but the most common and profitable route into property investment is as a developer and investor.

This means turning a house or parcel of land that you own into a potential goldmine that will begin to generate cash flow consistently so that you can soon begin to grow your portfolio.

Like any goldmine finding an investment property or land that nobody else has discovered is not as easy as it sounds unless you have the financial means to buy wherever you choose.

As a newbie property developer, you may have little choice other than to start with a property or land that:

1. Matches your budget
2. Gives you some money left over to build or renovate
3. Is located in the best area you can afford

If you have invested and the above works out well then you will be on the way to becoming the property investor who can make even better choices as a property portfolio is developed.

But all things considered, is property development really for you?

To become a successful property developer, you will need many of the skills usually associated with entrepreneurs and more besides. If you have always had a comfortable day job, then starting out as a property developer may be a steep learning curve.

You will need to take responsibility for the future direction of what will be a fully-fledged business and there are no hiding places when you are the owner of that business.

You will likely make mistakes along the way but I can tell you from experience that it will be immensely rewarding and you will soon find yourself becoming more financially savvy as a result of your experiences, so don't let anyone put you off if you are determined to make a go of it.

To start with, an ideal property developer could be a cross between a builder and Warren Buffet. If you are starting from scratch and don't have access to a large sum of money, then you will need to get your hands dirty with some practical DIY (or at least get a willing person to help you) and have the skills to look beyond the here and now and take calculated risks on future investment potential. You also need to be as ruthless with your time and resources as you are when cutting a deal.

The journey will be long and sometimes difficult but nobody ever got anywhere worth going in life without some challenges on the way. Good luck!

PART ONE:

STARTING OUT AS A PROPERTY DEVELOPER

I'm not going to dress this up in cotton wool for you - property development is hard. It will take up a lot of your time and you will encounter a certain level of stress at times. It can also be expensive.

Remember queueing up to go on a rollercoaster when you were a kid and reading all those reasons why you shouldn't go on the ride? It's the same when you decide to become a property developer. You can always play it safe and avoid the ups and downs but it's far more thrilling to have a go.

Unfortunately, as an adult, nobody is there to hold your hand or tell you what the pitfalls are.

Property development is for many people a venture into the unknown. So if you can agree with some or all of the following, property development may not be for you...

- I have little cash to invest
- I get stressed a lot over little things
- I don't have any DIY skills or know of anyone who can help me and I'm not prepared to do any of that kind of work myself
- I need a fast return on investment
- I'm never calm in a crisis
- I can't see myself devoting a lot of my time to developing property

- I want to see the world travel a bit before I start saving for the future
- I'm no good with maths and money matters. The thought of having to deal with finance and accounts scares me
- I dislike going to boring meetings about property investment

Aside from the above there are plenty of other reasons not to become a property developer but what about the reasons TO become a property developer, which is what we are really interested in and what this book will keep coming back to.

- I want to build something of my own for the future
- I don't want to work for someone else for the rest of my life
- I want to enjoy life in retirement and feel secure
- Earning a rising income in retirement sounds a lot better than relying on a fixed payment from my pension
- I want to have something to look forward to when I retire
- Owning a portfolio of properties means I can leave something behind for the kids
- I want to see how far I can go as a property developer

If you are reading this book, then you have already reached that point in life where you are considering what's next – what does the future have in store? The future is far from guaranteed for any of us but becoming a property developer means that you can build a future. You can eventually grow a portfolio of properties of your own which nobody can lay a claim to as long as you can cover the finance and make a profit when it is time to sell.

It is true of course that property values can fall as well as rise. Property development isn't for anyone who wants to get rich quick. Gambling is the best hope for those people, which leaves those of us who invest in property with an advantage. Property values tend to rise in the long term. There may be fluctuations over decades but the end point is still the same, the value of property has been consistently shown to increase over time. If you are prepared to put in that time and effort, the rewards can be huge.

Chapter 1

Laying the Foundations

If you want to build anything meaningful in life including a property portfolio, it has to start with a foundation. Getting the foundations right from the very beginning will help you right the way through your journey as property developer because you will always have that strong support to fall back on if you encounter difficulties.

One of the first things to consider is cash. Nobody ever became a property developer without having some cash even if it's a modest deposit. You will need cash to build or refurbish and property in any form doesn't come cheap if it's in the UK.

So how much money do you need to become a property developer?

You can't buy a property without money even if there are some organisations out there who tell you this is possible.

So if you don't have any money you have four options.

1. Get a job that pays better
2. Earn the money by setting up a business
3. Wait for a cash windfall

4. Find people who are cash rich and time poor who are willing to enter into some kind of joint venture

In my case I already had a business that provided the initial capital I needed to invest. Often, however, even if you do earn enough to consider becoming a property developer, getting hold of finance is usually the first step.

This may be in the form of a mortgage. You may have ambitious plans to buy a property you have seen that needs some attention and a location you think really couldn't be better. Then it comes to the meeting with the bank manager and the mortgage payments seem a little out of reach.

You might think that this development project will soon recoup the investment but wait a moment. Do you have any spare cash left over if anything goes wrong?

Unlike a straightforward property investment, a developer needs to take into account the cost of refurbishing and (or) building work because these two can really eat into cash, particularly if you are hiring tradespeople. If you have these skills already, then you will be at a distinct advantage over those who don't.

As a first step it is worth looking at a more modest property that falls well within your budget to protect yourself from any financial shocks on the way and, trust me, you can expect a few. Not having enough money can end up in a project stalling or worse still, it can lead to insolvency. It is far better to set a budget which will be the first and probably the most important part of your foundations at the beginning.

So now that you're ready to become a property developer let's look at the amount of money it takes to buy one.

The amount you spend on a development property depends of course on its location. You may even be considering a parcel of land on which to build on. Either way you can expect to pay at least a five figure sum.

The cheapest habitable property I have seen at the time of writing was a 2-bedroom end terraced house in Country Durham at a whisker under £20,000 which sold for nearly twice that amount back in 2004.

This should tell you all you need to know about the area in question. Property prices may rise eventually but you could be waiting a very long time in some areas of the UK thanks to the continuing legacy of the last big property market crash.

So while the price of this particular property may look tempting and it was even listed as an 'investment' you would need to be extremely careful and examine the area it is in and the reasons why it is so far below the average price of other terraced houses in the same area.

This was of course an extreme example but it highlights just how important it is to check things like price history which is readily available on websites such as Rightmove.

The ideal starter development property should be showing signs of its value increasing rather than declining over the long term. To do this it is better to look at prices over a decade rather than pay too much attention to short term fluctuations.

If you are lucky enough to find a project property in an area of rapidly rising property prices and have the means to purchase it at a knockdown price, then this can put you well on the road to success early on.

The same thing applies if you are looking to purchase land. Purchasing a parcel of land to build on is far cheaper than buying that same piece of land with a house sitting on it.

Because the value of that plot of land is less without a house built on it, you will have the opportunity to spend more time building the kind of property you want rather than do work on an existing house which may require as much labour and costs as building a property from scratch.

It all depends on any construction knowledge, any expertise you might possess in property development and the return on investment you are likely to receive for your efforts.

Where to look for financing for your development project

Most property books I have read leave this crucial bit out. They immediately launch into investing without addressing where the money is coming from. Finding out if you can get financing for your project is usually the first step before you even start making plans and looking for property or land to buy.

The money for property development usually comes from one or more of the following:

- Cash

If you have sufficient savings and, crucially, you can be confident of leaving some money in your bank account for a rainy day, then using your savings could be an option. You could also use your pension or income from other investments to fund the purchase.

If you are intending to use a large proportion of your cash, then it is worth getting some financial advice to make sure you are aware of the risks if things go wrong.

Property investment can be a risky business and using most or all of your money from the outset could leave you particularly vulnerable to unexpected costs.

- A mortgage

A simple buy-to-let mortgage is a common route into property development. Taking this option means you won't be spending all of your own money but you can expect to have to pay a sizeable deposit of typically 25% - unless you already have equity you can release in another property which we will cover in the next point.

You will also be paying a considerable amount of interest in the long term so shopping around for the best deal is essential as is making sure you are in a position to qualify. Banks are now far stricter on lending than they once were so your credit rating will need to be squeaky clean.

If you intend to use a mortgage, make sure that the monthly payments are affordable and fall well within your monthly budget. Finding a reputable mortgage broker is also very important. Check out my personal recommendations on www.nickfox.co.uk.

- Equity from your own home

It can be tempting to consider using your own home to help fund a property development project. If you have owned your own home for some time and have enough to cover 25% to 40% of the value of another property, then you could re-mortgage. If you have less than this amount in equity, then you may need to consider if re-mortgaging is worthwhile.

While it may seem like the better option, going down this route is not without risk or cost. You will of course be arranging two new mortgages which carry their own expenses in surveys, arrangement fees, solicitors' fees and so on. These can soon eat into your cash but depending on how long you have had your residential mortgage you may escape any early repayment charges.

How to start a property development business

My experience as a business owner was incredibly useful in giving me the necessary skills to become a full time property developer and investor. Without that experience it is unlikely that I would have developed a portfolio of over 200 properties.

A property development business like any business needs a plan. This plan should include what your goals are and how you plan to achieve them.

"Good fortune is what happens when opportunity meets with planning."

Thomas Edison

Buy to let or buy to sell?

Most property investors take the buy to let route where they invest money in property and generating a consistent return on investment over time. This is usually over five years or more. If you're looking at becoming a property developer, you can make a plan based around either buy to let or buy to sell.

Buy to sell is the riskier of the two unless you can be reasonably sure that the property market will still be in as good a shape as the property you are developing. The safer route is to buy to let because there are very few areas in the country that are immune to boom and bust if you are 100% reliant on achieving a set sale price that will more than cover your efforts developing a property with plenty left over for the next project.

If your business plan is based on a buy to let investment, then you will need to research and calculate the following:

- Likely rents in the area you invest
- Rental yields
- Tenant demand
- The type of property

I say likely because none of the above comes with a guarantee but with a little research, you can soon get an idea of the likely return you can make from your property development project over time.

If your rental yield is unlikely to be more than 5% then you should consider looking at an area where property prices are relatively low and rents are high. This is often the case in less fashionable towns that are close to areas where employment prospects are good.

The type of property you choose is vital if you want to make a success of property development. As in business, you need to provide what the market needs. If you're building a 4-bedroom property in an area predominantly populated by young professionals seeking 2-bedroom apartments, then you could find yourself with lengthy voids to contend with and compromises on the rent or sale price of the property. Build that same property in a picturesque location with an outstanding school and the opposite will be true.

Buy to sell will involve a projection of how much a property is likely to be worth when the development work is complete and whether there will be a buyer come exit time. You can then work out the profit minus the associated costs. Your profit from a buy to sell project should be in the region of 30% to make it worthwhile.

As with any business the plan should include financial projections as well as profit and losses that are anticipated along the way. Having good cash flow is essential so that you have enough cash available to cover development costs.

Hanging on to a job is probably a good idea or if you are not in employment, it is worth setting some emergency funds aside.

Finding the right kind of property

This really depends on what type of property developer you are. You could be the developer of a large scale property development that is being built from scratch on a plot of land, you may be considering a major refurbishment of an existing property or you may have a large-scale HMO project in mind.

As this book is geared to those starting out, we will assume that you are in the refurbishment bracket. In this case it is crucial that the property you choose is in the right location and the price is right as it is with all types of development projects.

If you remember anything from this book, remember that you make most of your money in property or land when you are buying and it is what you later do with that asset which determines how much icing you can add to the cake afterwards.

Research the Area

You will find plenty of information online about a particular area, local sale prices and rents on websites such as Rightmove and Zoopla. The right kind of property for you will be balanced between the price you pay, the value you can get out of it and your development budget.

Your aim should be to buy a property at a price that offers the best value in a particular area and this will always be a property in need of improvement. One important point to remember is that the cost of improving this property should be more than covered by the rent you are likely to receive or the amount you intend to sell it for when it is finished.

Invest in property that suits your budget and time

As a beginner developer it is better to opt for a property that doesn't have major structural issues or is too large even if those properties are available at a knock down price.

It is important to consider time as well as your budget. Turning a church into a residential dwelling only to find that the work takes 5 years to complete is not a good strategy if you want to build a portfolio.

Property development if you are going it alone can be hard work and hiring tradespeople can be expensive. Spending too long on a development project is simply a waste of time and money when you could be starting small and generating a profit sooner.

When it comes to location, you can find plenty of opportunities around the UK. The best areas to develop property will be in areas close to good schools and areas of high employment.

Locations near top graded schools (see Ofsted, Estyn (in Wales) are in big demand amongst anxious parents keen to send their children to the best schools. In these areas, family homes will be the better investments whereas in cities where space is more constrained and populated with young professionals, HMOS and other smaller dwellings will be more in demand.

Why cash flow is so important

Cash flow is as important to a property developer as it is to a business. Having enough of it is another matter. There may be times where a business is running at a loss due to having to pay bills or buy materials and equipment and it's the same with property development. In fact, it is a particular problem in property development because you will often be waiting a long time to see a return on your investment.

Even large property developers working on multi-million pound projects are stopped in their tracks when cash flow becomes a problem. They will then look to other sources of finance to get them over this hurdle but for a person who is new to the business of property development, getting hold of enough cash to complete a project can be a nightmare.

So generating cash flow while the building work is being done is essential if you want to avoid problems.

The top five things that can impact on your cash flow as a property developer are:

- Increases in bank interest rates
- Economic downturns that result in banks being less eager to lend money
- Unexpected costs
- Missed deadlines and delays
- Inability to sell or let the property which leads to arrears in finance payments

It has to be remembered that a building is one of the least liquid assets you can invest in. This means it is not as easy to sell and this is certainly the case when development work is taking place.

You are essentially tying up money to receive a longer term return on investment. This doesn't mean however that holding lots of cash is preferable to owning a property, holding lots of cash simply means you will be missing out on some potentially great future returns.

If you can maintain a good level of cash flow while the work is being carried out, then there is no reason why your development project will not be a success. Remember, property values tend to increase over time while the value of cash erodes due to inflation.

Chapter 2

Finding Your First Investment Property

If you find yourself in a good financial position, it is only natural you will be considering investing in property. You may be surprised how many people are doing just that. I know I was before I started out as a full time property developer.

I have made many friends who are building property portfolios and while most of them already had a clear idea where they would be investing there are a few who found it to be a daunting task in the beginning.

This is perfectly normal. Developing a property is a big commitment with many unknowns at the start.

If you are starting from scratch finding the right property to begin with can be a difficult task on its own. I can understand this because I felt exactly the same. This is where planning a strategy first can make things a lot easier as I will show you in this chapter.

Having a strategy allows you to separate your heart from your head, which is what you will need to do to keep a clear head. The key thing is to keep your strategy in mind at all times so that you don't get swayed off course by the many distractions you are likely to encounter.

It's easy to get distracted by how nice a property looks and let this influence your investment decisions. It's easy to find yourself confused by all the potential options available. Do you go for a flat, a house or build from scratch?

Having the right strategy means all of the above choices will be removed because you will have a clear view of the kind of investment property that fits with your aims and objectives. You will soon find out why one of the oldest sayings in property investment is as true today as it has ever been. Location, Location, Location.

The location you choose should be considered your own goldmine. It is a place you can return to again and again for properties that will be cash flow positive. It is a place where you won't have to work too hard to make a profit and just as importantly your goldmine should be an area you know and understand.

Like any prospector, when you start out as a property investor, you will be in the privileged position of being able to choose the goldmine that suits you best. For some property developers it's family housing, for others it could be student properties, HMOs or apartments.

Whichever you decide upon, it should be a market you know will provide you with cash flow, profits and enough left over to continue adding to your portfolio when all of your costs are considered.

Points to consider about your goldmine before you start digging

Supply and demand

At first glance this might sound easy. Find an area with a limited supply of properties and high demand right? Not necessarily. If you are hoping to expand your portfolio in the future, you will need to look a little deeper at the area(s) where you are hoping to expand your portfolio.

Property development can be turned into a full time business if you have enough properties. For property developers, houses are the product so there needs to be enough of them and a regular flow of deals.

The danger of investing in an area short of the kind of properties or available land to meet your investment goals is that your deal flow will eventually dry up forcing you to look elsewhere and leaving your resources spread too thinly across to wide an area. This can be a nightmare when it comes to managing your portfolio further down the line.

Employment prospects

The availability of jobs in your chosen area is critical to your success whether you are developing properties for sale or to let. The area you invest in doesn't necessarily need to be awash with employment opportunities, but there must be enough people around who can afford to rent or buy your property when the time comes to exit.

Growing employment and the imminent arrival of major employers to local business parks and nearby towns can all have a major effect on local property markets. It's easy to find out about future plans for a town by looking in the local papers or online where news will be released well before a major company or other large employer arrives.

Most town and county councils publish their development plans on their websites so this is definitely a good place to look.

Local Amenities

Looking for a potential goldmine isn't easy. The chances are the ideal properties to suit your strategy have already been taken in the best locations. So the challenge is to find a location that is as they say "on the up". An area with good primary and (or) secondary schools will be ideal if you are building a house for a family or looking to refurbish family-sized houses. If there is a large hospital nearby along with some nice restaurants and good transport connections, then your chances of success will be greatly improved. If on the other hand you are hoping to attract young professionals and students, then universities or close proximity to city and town centres is a must.

Flood Risk

Increasingly these days, given that rainfall levels in some parts of the country are now well in excess of what they have been in recorded history, flood risk is a critically important consideration.

Buying a property in an area with even a moderate flood risk can not only increase your landlord insurance premiums, but also put your whole property development business at risk if you don't have sufficient finances put by to ride out a storm. To avoid this, look carefully at national flood risk data which is freely available online. This will give you an idea of locations to avoid in your search for development opportunities.

Article 4 Direction and HMOs

One thing you really need to find out about if you are considering a HMO strategy is to make sure you are actually allowed to build or convert a house into a HMO. Local councils can sometimes impose a restriction known as an Article 4 Direction which prevents developers getting planning permission for houses that are rented to multiple tenants. You will find information on this from the local council.

These are just a selection of points to consider and you may find there are others depending on the type of property you are hoping to develop.

When is the right time to buy?

When is the right time to buy? This is the million-dollar question anyone who wants to become a full time property developer someday will be asking. If you are new to property development, then you will want to hit the ground running and make money as soon as possible.

Depending on who you go to for advice, some people will say there is a right time and some people will say there is a wrong time. You

42

will also hear that timing is crucial if you want to be able to profit from property investment.

I believe the right time to invest in property depends more on your own personal circumstances than what the market is doing or at what stage the market is at. Just because property prices are rising, this doesn't mean that now is the time to invest if you lack the finances for development or you don't have the necessary time to spend on building and refurbishing.

On the other hand, if you are already a buy to let investor looking to enter into property development full time, any income or capital losses can be offset against the rest of your portfolio, so timing when you buy a property isn't going to be too much of a concern.

Then there's your attitude to risk. As more people have used buy to let properties to help fund their retirement, property is sometimes seen as less of a risk than putting money in a pension!

It has to be said, however that you are not insulated from risk as a property developer and just as the rewards can be much greater than you would get from a pension, investing in the wrong place at the wrong time can leave you exposed to similarly high risks to match the potentially high rewards.

Assuming you have the means to invest in property and the time, then the right time to buy will be dictated by what you plan to achieve in your journey towards becoming a full time property investor.

Inevitably you will be using estate agents and they will often tell you that time may be limited to secure a property before it goes. This might suit you if you want to move quickly to gain a return on investment and you are confident enough about your choice of location that this will be possible.

The Property Market Cycle

A property cycle behaves much like an investment cycle. If you think of a cycle as a clock, then if 12.00 is the start of a cycle, this will be the time when property prices are at a base level in the locality. A property cycle typically lasts between 7 and 10 years depending on various economic factors.

Sounds simple doesn't it? Yet as we know, in life nothing worthwhile comes easy and the same is true in property development. If it wasn't many more people would be making millions out of property investment.

The only problem is that it is very difficult if not impossible to know for sure when property prices are as low as they can go. Many people were caught out when they thought the bottom had been reached back in 2009 when the general feeling was that house prices had fallen as low as they could go only to discover that they still had further to fall. What looked like a good deal then will have left many investors with losses from the outset.

The Bottom

This will be a level where the only way is up. For example, when house prices crashed in the UK in the early 1990s and in 2008, more than 30% was knocked off the value of many homes across the UK.

Following this crash price falls across the UK levelled off. Eventually a modest increase came in some areas. This levelling off is often called the bottom of the market.

This is a good time to look for distressed sellers who will be more than happy to sell to you while they are caught up in all the negative sentiment that follows a housing market correction. As Warren Buffett, the world's greatest investor once said "be greedy when others are fearful".

Investing in property at the start of a cycle has three big advantages for a property developer:

- Your budget stretches further and you can buy more property for your money. Even better if you are a cash buyer, this is the time when you can be most aggressive with your offer and often it's the time when you get the best deal.
- The risk of losing money as a result of a property losing value is low.

So now you know the advantages of timing your entry at this stage, now it's time to reveal some of the disadvantages.

One of the first is not knowing for sure when prices have reached rock bottom.

You may have seen this happen in the Spanish property market where there is such a glut of available holiday homes, prices have taken many years to recover. The bottom of the market was called several times in the intervening years only to see further deflation in property prices.

Developers and their agents will always try to talk up a market when sales have fallen in the hope that it will stimulate demand.

To avoid this, the best advice is to do your homework on a particular location. Some locations are of course better than others and if an area has a long history of significant house price inflation, there will be less risk involved because you can be confident that property values will begin to increase again sooner rather than later.

The other disadvantage of investing when prices are rock bottom is the availability of mortgage finance. Unfortunately, just at the time when property is priced as low as it can go, mortgage availability will have been tightened because the banks are still fearful of losing money. Though it has to be said those who are viewed as low risk by lenders will have an easier time borrowing and can do so at lower interest rates than those with questionable credit ratings.

Growth Phase

The growth phase is characterised by a change in sentiment from negative to positive. You will be hearing a lot about economic growth and house price increases in the news as well as the need for more housing.

The latter is often put forward as a reason for house price inflation even though it is rarely mentioned when there is a market slump. The banks buoyed by rising house prices soon start tempting in new customers with better mortgage deals and if you are a developer who is relying on finance from the bank to invest, now will almost certainly be a good time to buy.

Of course the other important thing about buying property for development in a growth cycle is that you can usually expect rising demand for rental properties as prices start to rise beyond the reach of potential purchasers in some areas of the country.

So if you time your entry in the growth phase you can expect:

- Rising property prices and a lower risk of a slump particularly early on in a new growth cycle
- More choice of mortgage products
- More demand for rental property

As with most things in life there are some disadvantages to timing your entry in a growth cycle. The first is that the rock bottom deals you could have enjoyed before prices started to increase will now be much harder to find, particularly in the more sought after areas of the country.

Peak of the cycle

At the peak of the property market cycle, prices will be reaching the point where they are unlikely to rise any further. This is where you will find the most heat in terms of property price inflation.

The only way is down from here as prices will have reached an unsustainable level and people will be more likely to cash in before the inevitable slump.

When you are attempting to negotiate a deal in this environment, people will be less willing than ever to drop the asking price because they will be under pressure to sell for the highest possible price so that they can trade up themselves.

The peak of a cycle is potentially the worst time to attempt to buy an investment property if you are developing a property for sale but if you are developing buy to let properties, rents will likely be pushed higher as many people are priced out of buying and the supply of potential tenants will also be hitting a peak.

So if you time your entry at the peak of the market you can expect it to be:

- The worst time to find discounted land and property
- Easier to find tenants with many people priced out of buying properties
- A time where risk is increased that there may be a market correction on the horizon

What goes up must come down

Unfortunately, as many people discovered in the noughties, property prices don't keep rising forever. Property - while not as volatile as stocks and shares - shouldn't be seen as a cashpoint or any kind of miracle investment.

To survive as a property developer, you must be prepared for any market corrections and have sufficient funds put aside to weather any storms that come your way. Relying on property price growth alone is a strategy that can soon end in disaster. When it comes to property development, slow and steady usually wins the race!

The important thing to take away is that as long as you stay up to date with your property education and the latest strategies it is possible to make money at any point in the property market cycle. This is true if you are new to buy to let or a seasoned property developer.

Choosing a property project that fits with your schedule

'Take time to deliberate, but when the time for action has arrived, stop thinking and go in.'

Napoleon Bonaparte

At the height of his powers Napoleon was a master strategist but even he ended up in exile on an obscure island because he didn't plan well enough for when his fortunes changed.

For the novice developer you may not be marching an army into a freezing Russian winter but you don't want to end up stripped of everything you own because you took a risk that didn't pay off.

On the other hand, there is a danger of missing out on an investment opportunity due to spending too much deliberating the pros and cons. Yes, you should definitely consider all the risks but quite often you may not have much time to buy your first development property before someone else does.

Part of becoming a successful property developer is learning how to take calculated risks and, more importantly, take action when it's required.

If you already have a plan in place that will give you an idea of the timescales involved in developing a property for rent or for sale, then you will avoid the pitfalls many amateurs encounter when they rush in.

Taking on projects that are too large or that don't fit in with family and work commitments can place considerable stress on everyone including family. There are plenty of cases of property developers who abandon projects because their projects seemed to go on and on with no clear end in sight.

What should you expect property development to involve?

At a basic level you will be developing or renovating a property to sell on or rent out to tenants when the work is complete. In the former case, once the work is finished on the property and you have found a buyer, then the work is done and you simply move on to the next project – assuming you sold the property with enough profit left over.

If you are developing property for tenants, then that property will require your ongoing commitment for the length of time you own it. To make a full time living you will need a portfolio of several properties to begin seeing the kind of returns that help you give up your day job or business.

What to Expect from your First Development Project

Starting your first property development project will certainly be a reality check. Looking back when I started out, I soon realised that the work involved can leave you stressed and it can demand more and more of your time. In other words it becomes very much like running a business and only those who have a very strong and positive work ethic will achieve success.

You also learn early on that what looks like great ROI on paper is not always the great return it appears to be when income tax and other expenses such as mortgage fees and repayments are taken out.

If you are to become a successful property developer, you will be more of a tortoise than a hare because it can take a several years to get the rewards for the work you put in at this early stage. There may of course be exceptions in a fast rising property market, but that kind of house price inflation hasn't been seen anywhere, apart from few major Western European capital cities, since the early to mid-2000s. In any case capital prices should not be relied upon for property investment success.

What's involved in the build phase? How much time do you need?

A lot depends on whether or not you will be doing the work yourself or hiring tradespeople. Hiring tradespeople can really eat into investment returns which is why you will see the vast majority of property developers doing work themselves.

There are plenty of builders and tradespeople who have decided to become developers and why wouldn't they be if they can cut out all the expense of hiring people like themselves?

As we have established, property development costs more than money, it costs a fair amount of time as well. So you may find you have the skills but not the time or if you haven't planned properly you may find that you take on too much. This can result in work not being done to the required standard and the extra cost of getting things put right. So you lose money and time you can ill afford to lose from the beginning.

Skills like plastering walls and ceilings are often necessary and they can take a bit of practice to get right. Another potential hurdle is maintaining motivation if you get home from work at 6pm and are then faced with five hours of plastering, painting or other jobs each night you can soon get worn out and disillusioned.

It might be better to find the right people at the right price to do those jobs for you.

The Importance of Planning Your Workload

Thinking you have the time is one thing, making sure you have the time is another and you will quickly discover this is the case with your first development project.

Imagine that you have just picked up the keys to your first investment property and you have all these ideas going through your mind at once. All kinds of tasks will probably need to be completed if you take on project from new flooring, rewiring, a new kitchen, adding an extension and so on.

With such a lot of things to take care of it is easy to go rushing in without thinking carefully about the order in which you will be working on those tasks. If you happen to be using a builder and other tradespeople this may well be taken care of as these people will hopefully have plenty of experience of working on property development projects.

Even so, if you have the budget, hiring a project manager to organise work is useful so that work is done in the right order and you don't have a situation where previous work needs to be redone – if for example flooring is damaged when the plumbers are called in.

If you are planning to do all or most of the work yourself then think very carefully about how the work should be done and in what order. If you are unsure there will be plenty of information available to help you in the following chapters.

7 Secrets of finding the right investment property

If you have ever attended a property seminar, you will hear people talking about the secrets of their success in property but do they ever show you where you should be buying to emulate their success?

It's unlikely anyone can give you an exact location where you should be investing because that will be decided by what your plans are and your current financial circumstances. If we decide that you are developing properties that you hope to fill regularly with tenants, then you will have different requirements to the luxury property developer who will be aiming at a much narrower market.

So with this in mind I am going to give the 7 secrets I have learned over the years as an investor.

Know your property type

It may sound obvious but there is a lot of misguided advice out there about which property type you should be focusing on. Many in the business will tell you that flats make the ideal investment but is that really the case? On the one hand flats can offer advantages to a developer if a house is converted into them because then you get to maximise the full value of the property by dividing it up into separate areas where you can charge multiple rents.

In this case flats are a very good idea in much the same way as HMOs, student properties and so on. If you intend to invest in a pre-built flat that is part of a larger block of flats owned and co-managed by other residents, then there are several pitfalls:

- Service charges can be high and are often set by majority decisions among residents.
- Ground rents can be a drain on your profits
- There may be unforeseen restrictions on the types of tenant you can allow
- There will probably be little scope for development work externally and little or no outdoor space.
- Flats are often occupied short term with a regular turnover of tenants. So you need to be prepared for voids

2 bedroom properties are often the easiest option because this type of property is more likely to attract a broad cross-section of potential tenants. Even people who live alone often appreciate the benefits of an additional bedroom they can use for guests or perhaps a home office.

Town and city centres usually make the best locations

If you are hoping to get your property let quickly, then it needs to be in areas where your tenants are going to want to live.

The biggest demand for rental property doesn't come from 30 somethings starting a family, it comes from young professionals and those who are renting property so that they can be nearer to their place of work.

Not surprisingly this sector of the population are the ones most likely to enjoy the hustle and bustle of life living in town or city centres rather than living in the country where there is little to do and getting to and from work involves queuing in traffic every day.

Easy transport links, particularly close to railway stations as well as close proximity to growing university campuses, large hospitals and other organisations that employ thousands of staff tend to make the best locations.

There may be times however where areas outside towns and cities attract large number of families seeking to rent or buy properties. In these cases, larger houses can bring attractive returns whether they are being developed for rent or for sale.

Who is your tenant?

If you plan to let your development property, it is vital you know what types of tenants you are hoping to attract. This probably sounds obvious but you would be surprised how often mistakes are made. The best strategy starting out is to aim for as broad a group of potential tenants as possible rather than targeting smaller niches. This will not only help you find tenants faster but also cut down potential void periods at times of the year when demand is low.

The importance of having the right layout

One thing you should never underestimate when you are either building a property or setting out to buy an existing property for refurbishment is the floor plan. A property should always allow for some flexibility to be appealing to tenants. Having one bedroom that is too small for a double bed in a flat and especially for a house can be a big turn off.

I remember going to view a property and being told by the agent that a box room could easily be used as a second bedroom if guests were prepared to sleep on a single mattress on the floor! You should never make compromises on a property, there will be plenty more available that suit your purposes better.

Make sure it has enough natural light

While there may be some people who actually like living like vampires in dark accommodation with little in the way of natural light, the vast majority of your potential tenants will appreciate an abundance of natural light. While you can get away with bedrooms being dark, it is nice to have natural light in kitchens and living areas. Having a good balance between the two is important and windows that allow everyone to see in might not be a good idea for people who like their privacy.

Find something out of the ordinary

You will always have an easier time selling or letting a property if it offers something extra over the competition. Avoid quirkiness but consider loft conversions, character buildings that stand out such as post-industrial building that have a bit of history behind them. The properties that turn people's heads will nearly always find tenants.

Avoid potentially noisy locations

Noise can be a particular problem even with the best double glazing fitted in some areas. Trust me one of the main questions tenant will ask you about is the level noise when they are viewing your property. Are you going to lie to them if there is a noisy pub next door and the property is on the main route to nightclubs on a Saturday night and schools on weekdays? You may get a tenant in short term by concealing the noise problem but you can expect a high turnover of tenants. It is far better to choose a development property where there is a healthy balance of local activity without the noise particularly late at night.

The importance of negotiating

"Start out with an ideal and end up with a deal."
Karl Albrecht

Nobody who ever made a fortune from property did so without negotiating on price. Effective negotiation is the foundation of any business and if you want to make it as a full time property developer you will need to learn this valuable skill from the beginning.

Negotiation will be your most potent weapon if you use it wisely. By wisely I mean you shouldn't simply use it to beat down the price and make silly offers that are never likely to be accepted.

One of the keys to successful negotiation in property is to treat your seller with respect. Any negotiation you make when you are buying property or land to build on should lead to a satisfactory outcome for both parties.

You set out with your ideal until you both meet at the right point where you get a good deal. It usually takes a bit of time to get to this point so some patience will come in handy because you can't expect a good deal to be presented to you without some negotiation otherwise the deal is unlikely to be as good as it seems.

Time is always your friend in negotiations. The seller may have other offers to begin with, which means it could take weeks or even months until that unmotivated seller becomes a motivated seller prepared to give you a good deal.

So how do I start negotiations?

The key thing to remember is don't rush in unless you really are confident that the price of your target property is too good to miss.

- Build a connection with the seller

It helps a lot if you are able to build some kind of rapport with the seller. They are more likely to give you the deal you want if they at least like you.

- Identify the pain

If someone is looking to sell their property, they are doing so for a good reason. If you can identify that reason early on and target that pain point, then you will be in the driving seat in the negotiation.

- Silence is good

Don't be afraid of silence. Letting people talk is the best way to find out information. Many novice negotiators talk about themselves and their needs without listening. If you listen long enough, you may get your deal handed on a plate.

- Unfortunately, you won't always get the deal you are looking for

Despite your best efforts at negotiation, you may not get the deal you want and you will be faced with the decision to adjust your own position on price or let the property go. In my experience it is better to simply move on to another deal but always leave the door ajar just in case they change their mind.

Enough About the Theory – What About the Numbers?

The most exciting part of the negotiation is the process of getting to the right price. The seller will have their position on price which could be £5,000 more than you are willing to pay so how do you close the gap?

The answer is in taking the right steps. Rather than start small with your offer, go the opposite and come in with your biggest concession. The chances are they will refuse this offer to begin with then after a time you can raise the offer but not by as much.

So you start with £1,000 and raise your offer by £500 and then when this is rejected raise it by £250. The seller is likely to cave in at the point where they think you have reached yours and their limit.

This is unlikely to happen all at once and offers will tend to be made over a period of weeks. So be prepared to take your time to get the deal you are looking for.

Chapter 3

Developing a Property

If we forget property for a moment and think of the word 'developer' or 'develop', the word is closely related to growth.

So property development is about growth. To get the best out of property development, you will need to grow an income from it and in most cases you will need to transform your properties so that they will continue to generate and build on that income.

Finding a property to develop is the easy part. Knowing what to do next entirely depends on why you are taking on a development project.

It could be that you are developing a property so that you can let it out to tenants. You may even wish to develop a property so that you can eventually live in it yourself.

For the purposes of this book, we can assume that the property you are developing is aiming to achieve the goal of a financial return.

So how do you achieve this goal?

It all comes down to desire. Desire is a word that links closely with growth and development. You can't grow or develop anything without having that magic ingredient - desire.

Let me tell you the story of a young guy called Frank.

Frank left school at 16 as people often did in his day without any qualifications that could support his ambition of getting a job in a retail store.

He applied for job after job and time and time again he was rejected until eventually he gained a job cleaning shop windows and arranging the display of goods. He was considered incapable of handling customers by his employers at the time.

Undeterred he continued to work and learn from those around him and the ways of the business until he eventually got to run a store of his own. He had built his skills to the point where he could generate an income.

Unfortunately, Frank's first attempt at running his own store failed – as did several others, until eventually he got the formula right.

So if we take Frank's early attempts to develop his business as a store owner, we see that it wasn't always easy and he first needed to learn lessons from those around him and when he encountered setbacks, he still had the desire to continue.

If we look at property development in the same way as building a business, then the same rules will apply.

Frank would go on to open 586 stores in the United States and become the proud owner of the tallest building in the world in 1913. You may recognise his surname Woolworth, which would become one of the most recognised brands of the 20th century.

This kind of story is repeated countless times among the people we see as the most successful in history. Henry Ford struggled in his early days in business, Bill Gates was a college dropout, Walt Disney was fired as a journalist for lacking imagination. What all these people had in common was the desire which drove them on to achieve legendary status in their fields.

Developing a property will almost certainly provide you with some challenges to overcome. If becoming a successful property developer for a living was easy and didn't involve some education and hard work, then everyone would be doing it.

It will probably stretch your abilities to the limit as a first time developer. You will also need to acquire the skills to organise and manage the development. Deal with tradespeople, perhaps gain investment for your project or manage your budget so that it doesn't get out of control or leave you with serious cash flow problems.

But as long as you keep the desire to achieve your goals as a property developer, you should be able to easily overcome any obstacles to the development of a portfolio that will generate more income than you ever thought possible at the beginning.

The following chapter will teach you what I have learned from hands-on experience of building a portfolio of more than 200 properties.

First Things First – Assessing The Property

My first experience of developing a property came as a child when my mother and I were forced to find alternative accommodation after we lost our static home to a fire. The intention then wasn't to find a property for development. It was more about finding a place to live quickly.

As luck would have it, this property turned out to be the start of something, even though I remember it being a complete wreck when we first came to view it. Most property developers will be familiar with buying properties that appear at first glance to be complete wrecks few other house buyers would touch with a barge pole.

If you want to be a property developer, you will certainly need vision to succeed!

Yet it is often the case this type of house will become the foundation of a property portfolio with a bit of hard work. One thing I would add however is that not all wrecks are necessarily suitable for a development project.

You will still need to assess a property for its potential just in case the cost of renovation outweighs the likely return you will get from it. I will cover more on gross development value in the next section but if we start with the basics of assessing a property there are a few basic areas to focus on first before making a decision.

How much scope is there for development?

This may be an obvious question but one that is not easy to answer without a full inspection. Development projects come in many different forms. You may be considering a former council flat, a period house, or a rundown terraced house.

Whatever the property type, if you are developing a property it will require changes to make it desirable for tenants. Making those changes in most cases will be easy, if you have the skills or have someone available to help you with the work. What you can't change are restrictions on development work that come with some properties.

If you can't knock out walls to open up space in a flat or there are issues with planning permission, then these can create unnecessary headaches. It will be far easier in the long run to look for a project where you can really add value than be forced to work within boundaries.

There are always plenty of properties available that won't restrict your ambitions, so simply move on to the next opportunity if the house or flat you have found doesn't quite fit with your vision.

Is it possible to extend?

If your first property development project is a house then depending on where that house is located, there may be room to add an extension. Many older properties have huge gardens which are nice for the people living in them but an opportunity missed for a developer.

Assuming you can get planning permission, there may be scope to add an extension that will transform a property and raise the level of rent tenants will be paying to live in it. The more space you can add, the more valuable your asset will become both in terms of its desirability as a rental property and when it's time to sell.

Parking

One of the most important aspects of any property is parking. If you can provide off-road parking for your future tenants, then your property is likely to be far more desirable than living in a house where each day is spent trying to reverse into tight, on road spaces.

The vast majority of the population owns a car of some sort so providing it with a secure home on your property should be a priority where possible. There may even be additional space for more than one car, which would be ideal if you are investing in a house you expect to be letting to multiple occupants.

One note of caution is to look into planning permission if you plan to add a driveway or replace an existing one. Building a driveway onto main roads will require both planning permission and specialist contractors with licenses to do the work, which can be expensive.

Remodelling

Many older properties can benefit from some form of remodelling, even some more recent examples. You may find, for example, the house has a tiny kitchen separated from the dining room by a wall.

Simply knocking out a dividing wall can really open up a space and make it more in keeping with contemporary kitchens your prospective tenants will find more appealing.

Undertaking this sort of work will require some advanced building skills and you may also need a plumber and electrician to re-route pipes and electric cables. All of this can be costly so expect to be investing a four figure sum for this work alone if you are unable to do the work safely yourself.

Knocking a supporting wall out can have disastrous consequences, so it is well worth paying to get the job done by a professional.

Loft Conversions

If your development property is located in an area where extending isn't possible or there are planning issues restricting development externally, then a loft conversion may be possible.

Loft conversions can add an extra bedroom to a property or perhaps a study. In a busy city adding this extra space can raise the level of rent you can charge your tenants and increase your return on investment.

One thing to bear in mind is cost. Some lofts may not be suitable for conversion due to the cost of meeting building regulations. You will need at least 2.2 metres of headroom in your loft and that is after you have added insulation and flooring.

It is possible, depending on the type of loft conversion, to raise the height of your loft or extend usable space which can create an additional bedroom. Beware however that the costs can sometimes outweigh the benefits.

While the above renovations can be radical solutions, it may also be the case that all your property requires are some cosmetic changes. Often small changes may be all that is needed to add value to your investment.

Calculating your Gross Development Value (GDV)

You may or may not be aware what is meant by gross development value (GDV). Many first time property developers will also be unaware of what this simple calculation is, leaving them exposed to increased risk when they purchase land or property for development.

The calculation involves coming up with a reasonably accurate figure of how much a property will be worth on the open market when all the works are complete. This estimate should be as close as possible to reality and not based on some inflated calculation based on the potential of a given area.

While many property investors benefit from investing in areas that are unfashionable, this can be a risky strategy when the area doesn't quite live up to its potential. The latter can be heavily influenced by economic climate and this is notoriously hard to predict, even in the medium term.

If your projections are flawed this increases the risk of your development project failing or worse still falling at the first hurdle and putting you in a position where your losses leave you no longer able to afford to add to your portfolio.

So I cannot stress enough that your aim should always be to make a profit. Calculating your GDV will enable you to:

a. Assess what your property will be worth and the profit you can make on a sale

b. Calculate the likely rental value and the long term profits you are likely to generate from your tenants.

Calculating Your GDV

The calculation is simple as long as you are prepared to look carefully at comparable properties in the local area. Depending on your development aims this could be an assessment of the local rental market or transactions if you are planning to sell when works are complete.

You will find that not all locations are the same when doing this research. Some areas will have high rental demand, yet sales will be few and far between. These tend to be less fashionable towns that offer plenty of employment but little in the way of what could be seen as a good quality of life relative to other towns.

On the other hand, you could have locations that attract both high demand for rental property and high demand from property buyers. Family houses close to good schools typically fall into this bracket.

Either way you should be able to get a very detailed idea of likely rent and (or) sales prices free from websites such as Rightmove and Zoopla. You can even monitor certain postcodes and be alerted of transactions regularly.

Calculating your profit using GDV

Once you have researched your area fully, you can then use the following formula to calculate your likely profit:

$$Profit = GDV - (Construction + Fees + Land)$$

Your profit is what you anticipate will be the value of your property on the open market today when it reaches completion minus your acquisition and construction costs.

If your calculation comes up with a positive number allowing some margin for error, then the risk of your development failing to generate a return are reduced.

Perry's Valuation Tables

If you want to go even deeper into the process of assessing your property's investment potential, then a series of investment tables produced way back in 1913 may help.

You might be thinking, how could a bunch of tables produced at the beginning of the 20th Century help me today?

Like all the best inventions, Richard Parry's Valuation and Investment Tables remain an indispensable part of a property professional's tool kit. Parry's tables help examine the history of property investment and use it to your advantage.

Parry's Valuation and Investment Tables can help you analyse how inflation can affect investments over time and the type of financial climate that would be most beneficial for your development venture.

This can not only help you manage risk - it might also maximise your profits. The book can be purchased for around £15.

7 Things To Expect In A Typical Property Development Project

For the purposes of this book we can assume that you are about to start out in property development so what you can expect to encounter will be very different to an experienced developer with a track record of several projects.

As a novice property developer, there will be two likely routes you take. One is to build from scratch and the other the renovation or refurbishment of an existing property. While it's impossible to predict what particular challenges you will face with your development project we can assume that you will be faced with the following 10 areas of concern.

1. Building and planning regulations

Whether you plan to build a house from scratch or renovate an old council flat or convert a house into a HMO, you will need to familiarise yourself with local planning regulations. Knowing what you can and can't do with your property should be one of the first things to look into before starting work.

2. Appointing an architect or designer

Having someone with the ability to transform a property so that tenants or buyers will find it desirable can almost certainly add value to your investment and development project. Whether it is useful for your particular project will depend on your investment aims.

If you are developing property in an area where demand for rental property is high, then going to the extra expense of creating a property with wow factor may not be worth it.

If it won't make you any extra profit on your investment, then the money will be better used elsewhere although you may still need an architect for more complex refurbishment projects.

3. Getting quotes and managing budgets

If you are hiring builders and other contractors to do the work for you, then getting hold of at least three quotes for each task can save you money. Quotes can vary wildly, but it is also important to consider the quality of their past projects and not only the price. Each tradesperson will also need to come along and do an inspection to make sure their prices are accurate and your initial costs don't spiral out of control.

4. Getting your hands dirty?

There's nothing like getting involved in the nitty gritty of your first property development project. It can even provide some relief or escape from all that planning, paperwork and money management. If you have DIY skills, it can also save you a significant amount of money, which is why you often find tradespeople turning their skills to property development!

If you don't have these skills, then anyone can join in with a bit of labouring work as long as you're not getting in the way of work being done. One thing you shouldn't do is attempt complex construction projects, or building work such as knocking down walls without the relevant skills unless you are confident you know what you are doing.

Sometimes trying to do all the work yourself can end up taking you years of hard work when you could be leaving that to others and focusing on your financial returns.

5.   Project management challenges

Starting out on a development project will in most cases be challenging, not least the amount of organising that needs to be done. You may choose a project manager to manage all this for you and more often than not you will eventually anyway as your development portfolio expands, but if you prefer to do it yourself, prepare yourself.

You will need to keep the lines of communication going with the people working on site to make sure deadlines are being met as well as make sure materials are being delivered on time and in the right order. If you are building a property from scratch, a large proportion of your time will be spent sourcing materials and suppliers.

6.   Sorting out insurance

If you are managing a development project, then you will need to ensure that you and your on-site team have insurance that will cover for any accidents that may happen on site. Your contractors will probably already have contractors' liability insurance but there is no harm in checking to be on the safe side.

7.   Handling Waste Material

Whether you are building a brand new property or remodelling an existing house, you will be creating a lot of waste material and rubble. You will need to hire skips and try to keep waste building material to a minimum to reduce the cost of disposal. You will find that some materials like brick can be recycled and other rubble can be used in garden landscaping projects, so don't be afraid to hang on to some materials that may come in handy.

Why Managing Time Is Critical To Success

If there is one thing that you need to become a property developer, it's time. Unfortunately, you won't have much of it when it comes to getting your property ready to rent or sell, so learning how to manage it effectively is critical.

Some of the biggest issues that crop up during building work are:

- Delays in getting supplies delivered
- Missed deadlines
- The weather!

It takes just a few months for a construction firm to build a house if the parts used to build them are standardised. It will take significantly longer to build a custom house from scratch. Renovating a property as long as it is in a reasonable state shouldn't take longer than it would take to knock it down and rebuild, so you will need to choose the project that is right for you.

If you work full time and take on a property that needs significant renovation and refurbishment work, you could be setting yourself up for years of work and lost opportunities. I have met property developers who have done just that and ended up trying to sell a property just to rid themselves of the burden.

This can be a disastrous start for anyone hoping to make an income from property so an accurate assessment of work involved is essential to plan how much time you have and roughly how long your project will take to start giving you a return on investment, which is what it's all about.

The most popular route for property developers starting out is to find a house or flat that needs a bit of renovation or remodelling work. Older council flats and houses can hide a lot of potential for investors.

How much time it will take to transform a property into one that will appeal to tenants depends on the age of the property and its condition. Often all that is required is the introduction of a modern kitchen and bathroom, new flooring and a few coats of paint.

If you can find a property that just requires cosmetic changes for a good price relative to comparable properties in the local area, then you can factor in the cost of basic changes into the price you are willing to pay to buy the property.

If the work is extensive on the other hand and you lack the skills for work such as plastering, knocking out walls and fitting new kitchens, you may need to allow for as much as £10,000 – £15,000 to hire tradespeople and buy the materials you need and also factor in the time this work will take.

If you are taking out a mortgage to fund your buy-to-let investment, then you will be making a loss for each month you will be working on the property, so it's important that the time you may lose is compensated for by the rent you expect to receive when all the work is complete and your tenants can move in.

As you become more experienced as a property developer, then you will have a better idea of the timescales. This will help you on future projects as you expand your portfolio.

9 Useful Skills You Need To Become a Property Developer

Everyone has talents, some of them can remain undiscovered. When you start out as a property developer, you probably will discover talents you never thought you had. As well as the financial rewards you may receive in the future, gaining experience in all kinds of skills will always be useful.

You will find however that we all have limits when it comes to certain aspects of property development. We can't all be good accountants, plasterers and plumbers, but here are 10 skills you can acquire if you are determined enough.

1. Basic construction knowledge

If you want to become a property developer, even a little construction knowledge can be a tremendous help. While you don't have to be a bricklayer or structural engineer, knowing the difference between a stud partition and a load bearing wall as well as being able to spot potentially expensive faults in a property can save you a lot of money.

2. Basic Accountancy

Accountancy is another vital skill to have when you are a property developer. Managing budgets, income and your ins and outs while the development work is taking place will prevent overspending and ensure that you stick as close as possible to your budget. You will need to keep your gross development value in mind at every stage of the development work so that the work you are doing doesn't end up costing more than you're likely to make on the property.

3. An understanding of legal issues and jargon

As long as you have a good conveyancer, most of the legal issues surrounding your property will already have been settled but it will still be worth doing some background reading on issues such as leasehold and freehold. Over the years I have found that being able to ask the right questions and go above and beyond those asked by regular house buyers. Even an experienced conveyancer might miss potentially problematic issues with a property, which can come back to bite you further down the line.

4. Good communication skills

Having good communication skills are essential to your property development success. There are so many people to communicate with not only in your development team but also when it comes to managing your investment properties in the future.

Good communication isn't just about one-way traffic either, you will also need to be a good listener when you are handling and managing a building project. First you will need to make sure that your plans are being followed by tradespeople.

Sometimes your tradespeople may have their own opinions on how work should be done but this may not always suit your plans. In these cases, you don't always need to follow their advice if you are confident that you are right.

5. Management skills

Being a good manager is essential to ensure you get the best out of your development team. While some developers will do a lot of the work themselves when starting out, there are bound to be times when you need other people to help you accomplish your goals, particularly on more complex construction projects. Regular site meetings are important even if your development is small in scale. Getting together with your team even if it's a small one can ensure that the building work is done efficiently and on time.

6. Negotiating

We have covered negotiation in some depth in earlier chapters but is worth mentioning here too. To get the best deals on anything including how much your tradespeople are willing to work for and the price of materials requires negotiation. If you were able to negotiate a good price for your property at the beginning, then you should now be reaping the rewards.

7. Problem Solving

Anyone who thinks they won't encounter any problems when developing a property is deluding themselves. Unless you can afford to take your time on property development which let's face it is highly unlikely, then you will be working long hours rushing to get the work done. You will also need to solve any problems that arise on site and in scheduling, so having some problem solving ability will be useful and particularly so if you are tackling some or all of the construction work yourself.

8. Marketing

Unless you have a good estate agent lined up to help you advertise your property, then it is a good idea to brush up on some essential property marketing skills. These will generally involve the Internet as that is where most people will be looking nowadays. Some estate agents will be pro-active in helping to market your property, others can be slow.

You should be thinking about advertising your property before the completion date so that you have someone lined up ready to move in. Photos will be required if you plan to advertise the property yourself and you will find that there are plenty of websites including Gumtree where you can advertise your property for rent for free.

9. Motivation skills

All those long hours can take their toll, so it is important to be able to keep yourself motivated during the project. Often it may not be possible to devote all your time to developing your property as there may be conflicting demands on your time from family to work commitments. To stay motivated it is important not to push yourself too hard and be able to take a bit of time out now and again to relax and recharge.

Assembling a team to do the work for you

The size of your property development team and the expertise you need will largely depend on the scale and complexity of what you are taking on. There are plenty of property developers out there who get by largely by themselves with a bit of expert help here and there.

Eventually, as your portfolio increases in size and the scale of the work with it, you will inevitably need a team of people around you who can handle all the work as your development portfolio grows. There simply won't be time to handle everything by yourself.

When I started out and purchased my first house, the refurbishment side was hard work and meant long hours preparing the property. Nonetheless I found the whole process enjoyable and the satisfaction of seeing the house increase in value made it all worth it. I was hooked and went on to add many more properties to my portfolio.

Since those early days, however, I began to realise how much I needed a team to help me. Property development is when all said and done a business and everyone knows that no business can be successful if the founder does all the work!

So here are the people I found most useful when building my property development business:

Builder

Having a good builder to call upon is essential not only when it came to preparing each property for rent, but also all the issue I would need to deal with later on. Houses and flats start to look their age after a few years just like anything else so having someone reliable to help you with general maintenance of your properties is very important if you don't want your tenants becoming disgruntled with leaks, crumbling plaster and so on.

Electrician

The electrician is the tradesperson I probably end up calling the most and the importance of getting all the wiring checked and fitted correctly is vital. The last thing you want is for a house to end up on fire due to faulty wiring.

Plumber

Replacing bathrooms and fixing plumbing certainly keep my plumbers busy. Plumbing jobs can often be difficult and time consuming so while I can handle the basics, I tend to leave this to the experts.

My Accountant

It would be virtually impossible for me to manage my portfolio without my accountant. The more your portfolio grows the more you will need help managing the financial aspects such as taking in rental income, paying tax and making sure the books are balanced .

Estate agent

Another indispensable part of my team is the estate agent who has excellent knowledge of the areas I operate in. Having this vital knowledge to hand cuts down on the time it takes to source new development opportunities and ensures that I am among the first to hear about property with potential.

Surveyor

Knowing a good surveyor is important so that you don't end up buying property that has major structural issues or other problems that may not be immediately apparent at the time. Being able to sort the good properties from the bad ones is one of the keys to success in property investment.

Depending on your own ambitions you may need to appoint additional people to work as part of your team including architects, a project manager and so on.

Chapter 4

What Type of Property is Best?

The easiest route into property investment is to purchase either a house or a flat. There are of course other alternatives such as hotels and student blocks if you happen to have a million or so to spend on buying land and building on a large scale but that is a whole different level of development that would fill another book.

For me, houses and houses of multiple occupation (HMOs) have proved to be the best long term investment compared to the alternatives. There are however other alternative housing types that fall within the broad definition of residential property and the type of property you choose should be closely aligned with your investment aims.

Whether or not you decide to go for a house or flat, it is important to be aware of the risks and benefits of each so that you can make an informed decision. You will often find that property developers tend to specialise in one or the other and stick to what works for them.

To help you decide whether a flat or a house is right for you, here are some of the advantages and disadvantages of each:

Advantages of Houses

- Houses generally offer higher capital growth than purchasing individual flats.
- Houses can often be extended or turned into HMOs or flats if they are big enough. This can dramatically improve your potential rental returns.
- More often than not a house will be freehold rather than leasehold, so the sale process is often less complicated and you will have more control.
- You won't need to seek permission for basic development work apart from alterations requiring planning permission.
- You will be the only person responsible for the property, so you won't need to answer to a management committee or abide by rules set by the freeholder of the flats or other occupants.
- If you buy a family house, your tenants will generally be longer term than those opting for flats, so frequent void periods will be less likely.

Disadvantages of Houses

- Houses will cost you more up front than flats.
- They are a lot more work. Houses have more rooms and floors than your usual 2-bed flat, so this will really add to your preparation and maintenance costs.
- If the house has a garden, you may have extra work to do keeping it tidy. In my experience the majority

of tenants aren't keen gardeners, particularly the short term ones.

- You're more likely to be accommodating families with children and as anyone who has had children knows, younger kids can cause damage to property by doing things like writing on walls.
- You will almost certainly need to pay stamp duty when buying a house for investment purposes.

Advantages of Flats

- One of the great things about buying into a block of flats is that the building will either be managed by residents or a management company. This means the external areas and common parts will be looked after.
- Flats in town and city centres are in high demand among young professionals. They are often the first step on the ladder for those who don't want the higher bills associated with a house.
- The amount of maintenance required will be far less than with a house.
- You probably won't have much of a garden to look after.
- Flats are often worth a lot less than houses in the same area, yet rents can be comparable. This means your potential yield will be higher than with a house.

Disadvantages of Flats

- More often than not you won't own the freehold.
- If you don't hold the freehold, the chances are you will be paying a ground rent every year for the duration of your ownership. This is another ongoing expense that will be taken away from any profit.
- If the flat is part of a block you will end up paying regular service charges that cover maintenance of the common parts. Service charges can be expensive for some units.
- Your market will generally be limited to young couples and singles. Therefore, tenants will often only stay in the property for 12 months and this will mean extra effort finding tenants to replace them. Renting a flats is often seen as a stepping stone rather than a permanent solution for young professionals.
- While you can make money on the eventual sale of a flat, it could be a long way off in some parts of the country. The value of flats simply doesn't go up as fast as houses in my experience.

Whether you choose a flat or a house is largely down to what suits your risk profile best. Flats are low maintenance compared to houses and you can quickly build a portfolio in some great locations.

Houses on the other hand have much better capital growth potential in the long term and you don't have the headaches of dealing with leaseholds and resident committees. So if like me you like to be in full control of your property development business, then houses are on balance the better option.

You may have already decided on the issue of a house or flat but within these you will also be faced with other types of property to consider, which we will cover in the following sections.

Wrecks and Renovation Projects

A good renovation property available at a knockdown price is a property developer's dream. My own property adventure began with a wreck and if I was to go back to the beginning of my journey as a property developer, I would opt for the same house again.

You won't need to spend much of your hard-earned cash buying a wreck and if the construction work is limited, you can soon start making money.

Unfortunately, not all property renovation projects will be simple and you will be competing with other investors who are looking for similar properties. The structural shortage of property in the UK in the best areas is something of a blessing and a curse in this regard. While selling and letting a property in these areas is easy, finding them is another matter.

According to research from the empty homes agency, an estimated 280,000 homes are standing empty in the UK. If we assume that not all of these are in prime spots for buy-to-let investors, then the number of wrecks suitable for renovation will be significantly less than this figure.

More than 2 million buy to let loans have been approved since 1999 and there are an estimated 1 million BTL landlords in the UK at the moment, which suggests that there will be plenty of competition for property and shrinking your options even further.

This is one of the reasons why I recommend a getting a good estate agent to source opportunities for you as and when they arise. Another way is of course to do your own research if you are really keen on uncovering a gem.

Finding Derelict Properties With Development Potential

One way to find property that is under the radar is to look around at plots of land for sale. These may already have derelict buildings on them, which can with some work be transformed into profitable investment properties.

Aside from searching on the usual websites like Right move and local estate agents, there are also websites set up dedicated to these plots of land. The majority of what you will find will probably be better knocked down but you never know, there could be a house worth recycling.

Old Pubs

It may be sad to witness the demise of the good old British pub but there is at least the consolation of converting abandoned ones into large residential dwellings, even if there is less chance of enjoying a nice pint of beer or a glass of wine. There are even specialist pub investment brokers who can help you source development opportunities.

Historic Buildings

Depending on where you live in the country, there may be opportunities to work on renovating historic buildings including those that may be at risk. This is a very particular niche however and more suitable if you have a passion for this type of project.

It is unlikely that this type of building would make a good development project from a cash flow point of view. Repairing original features can be expensive and you will have all sorts of restrictions on what you can do with the building.

Remember, becoming a successful property developer is as much about making sound financial decisions as it is about the property you buy.

Period or New Property – Which Is Best?

This can be a difficult question to answer. One thing I would say to you is, most of the people who ever made money from buy-to-let are buying older properties they do up to either sell or rent out, even if they are not necessarily what you might call 'period' properties.

Period Property

Period property is of a course a broad term that can be interpreted in different ways. A 1970s or even a house built in the 1980s could be defined as a period property. What I would think of as a period property however are the kinds of buildings you find in prime areas of cities and towns around the UK.

These are your typical Georgian town houses, or buildings dating back to the Victorian era which includes converted mills and breweries in the UK cities that have found new purpose as trendy apartments for city dwellers.

The reason you are more likely to find these types of buildings in prime spots is obvious when you think about it. As cities have grown and expanded rapidly in the last century, the buildings that have escaped demolition date back to when towns and cities were far smaller. As cities have grown, these buildings have become part of the fabric of city centres up and down the country.

Many of them are also protected which along with competition for commercial office property and scarcity of development land has pushed up prices for period property.

New build properties on the other hand, or those built in the last 15-20 years are often found in secondary locations, even if they lie within commuter belts.

So the appeal of investing in period property is in the capital growth potential over time and also the extra rent you can charge on a property that offers tenants closer proximity to the office, free city or town centre parking and easy access to entertainment and night life.

If you have the funds to accommodate the extra cost a period property that can be converted into modern accommodation suitable for young professionals should be able to attract a premium rent.

With period properties in scarce supply, they will often be more desirable for tenants too, particularly the ones who are seeking a bit of character. High ceilings, and nice big windows are often a feature of older period properties, which make them ideally suited to young trendy professionals living and working in the city.

All of these factors make period property appear to be a good investment. However, there is as always a downside. Buying in a prime location means that you will be paying a lot more for your property than you would if you were buying somewhere further out from an urban centre.

Older period properties may also require a lot more renovation work than newer properties, particularly older industrial properties that need to be completely transformed for residential purposes.

Modern properties and new builds

Modern properties and those built within the last 40-50 years as well as newer properties are the ones most likely to be purchased by a property developer.

While investors may opt to buy a new build and be prepared to wait for capital growth, a developer will be more concerned with developing the raw product into a saleable and rentable property.

This may for example be an ex council flat in an up and coming area of a city, a terraced house on a busy urban street or in some cases a detached house in the suburbs.

In most cases the newer the property, the less work will be required to develop it and this is important for those who have a limited budget. A look around most estate agents is bound to turn up plenty of properties that could be classed as recent, yet requiring modernisation.

Most of the work on newer properties is likely to be cosmetic or may involve knocking out walls to make spaces more open-plan in keeping with today's preference for space.

Energy performance scores are also likely to be higher on newer properties. With energy efficiency becoming increasingly more important to both tenants and buyers, replacing boilers, insulation and other improvements can add significantly to your costs.

Another advantage of buying newer property is that compared to period property in a similar area, the price is likely to be lower. Unfortunately, this also means that capital growth is likely to be less than that you would get from a more appealing period property.

According to studies by estate agents, period properties experience as much as 30 per cent greater capital growth than new builds each year when they are located in similar areas of a city.

To get the best deal on newer properties, it is wise to wait for at least ten years to make sure you are not contributing towards the buyer premium that is typically added on to new properties.

Whether you are opting for a period or newer property, always make sure you have a comprehensive survey before buying. Newer properties can hide problems just as well as older ones.

Converting a house into flats

So far we have looked at basic property developments projects aimed at individual tenants and families. Another option is to buy a larger houses and convert them into blocks of flats.

The benefits of this are you can multiply your rental returns and potentially make more money than you would from the property let as a whole house. In areas where there is high employment and rents for property are high, people are more likely to consider living in a house that has been converted into flats.

Starting out on a development of this kind however can be daunting. It will almost certainly involve a lot of work and extra expense complying with current legislation as well as making sure your tenants will be comfortable.

3 essential steps to take before turning a house into flats

Transforming a property into a block of flats is not for the faint hearted and you may need extra funds to make it possible, but as long as you follow the next 3 steps, finding the right property should be easy:

1. You first stop should be local estate agents who can advise you on local rental demand. Is it the right area to introduce a new block of flats or is it already saturated with flats? If supply of rental property is tight then your chances of void periods will be much lower.

2. Do the maths. If you divide a property up into individual flats will the likely rental return more than cover your development costs?

3. Research the demographic. Is your property aimed at students or young professionals? The latter will be more discerning about where they live, but increasingly students too will have the option of high spec student flats that are furnished with the latest modern appliances.

When you have considered all of the above and decided on your property, you will then need to seek planning permission. You should never buy property with the intention to convert it into flats without first checking that it is allowed in your location. If you can secure a property that already has planning permission, then this will be a bonus.

If the property doesn't have planning permission in place, it is worth doing some research into the area to see if other properties have been converted into flats. You should also have a good architectural understanding of the property you buy for this purpose.

You will need to follow current building regulations as well as understand how much work and cost will be involved in the conversion. You should expect the work to cost somewhere in the region of £40,000 for the average conversion because you will need to work on the following:

- Install sound insulation between flats. Nobody wants to live in a noisy apartment.
- Make alterations to existing plumbing so that it can be split between flats.
- Also split electrical wiring between flats.
- Install fire protection and provide adequate fire escapes.
- Make structural changes

Renovating Houses for Multiple Occupation (HMOs)

Another area you can choose to look at as a property developer are houses of multiple occupation, otherwise known as bedsits or HMOs. In case you are not familiar with this type of property it is defined as a property with at least 3 tenants who pay rent and share usage of kitchen, bathroom and toilet facilities.

This type of housing is popular with many tenant types, young professionals being the ideal, who are happy to share a house in return for lower housing costs. HMOs are one area I have specialised in over the years and I have written several books on the subject so I won't go into too much detail here other than to define how a HMO might fit your development strategy.

HMOs are well known to generate yields well above those you would get from a standard buy to let property. You will essentially be carving up a house so that three or more people can share it and pay rent.

The HMO can be a win win for both tenants and landlords. The tenant gets to save money by sharing with other rather than renting a whole property with extra rooms they may not need.

A HMO can be an ideal solution for people who work in a city and need to rent temporary accommodation. Rent can be less than half what it would cost to rent a whole property.

For landlords, instead of buying a 3-bedroom property, renovating it and then putting it up for £550 rent, they can turn that same 3-bedroom property into a HMO and let each room for £325 a month. The income is multiplied and so is the rental yield.

So why then isn't everyone turning houses into HMOs?

While the maths may look simple, your costs are increased when you become a developer of a HMO. First of all, you may need a mandatory licence if the house is occupied by more five or more people and has three or more storeys.

You will need to contact the local council if you are planning to turn a house into a HMO to find out if you need a licence. Licence fees can be more than £800 and you will also need to be approved to manage a HMO. Applications can be refused if the council believes a person isn't fit to be managing this type of housing.

Who would benefit from a HMO strategy?

- If you want to take the short cut to creating wealth from property, you won't find a better vehicle than HMOs.

Your returns will be multiplied compared to standard buy to let properties.

- If you plan to be hands-on with the management and don't mind the extra work dealing with lots of people and their tenancy agreements.
- If you are purchasing a large house and rent in the area doesn't quite make it worthwhile return, then converting the property to a HMO can raise the yield significantly.

A HMO strategy may not be for you if:

- You don't have a lot of time to spare e.g. property development isn't a full time endeavour.
- If you prefer to sit back and let other manage everything for you, you may not get the best returns as a passive investor in HMOs.
- You hate paperwork and dealing with lots of tenants, many of who can be short term.

One important thing new investors and developers should bear in mind is the extra workload of HMOs. This shouldn't be underestimated and for people new to development, it will be a steep learning curve and more costly in terms of preparation.

Once a portfolio has been established, however, it can be much more rewarding than taking the conventional buy-to-let route. If you want to read more about a winning HMO investment strategy You can learn all about it in my book HMO Property Success which is available to purchase from my website www.nickfox.co.uk or from Amazon.

Developing Student Properties

Student properties have become big business in recent years. As a developer starting out, student property can be the perfect sector to begin with demand being so high at the moment in many university towns and cities.

You will be competing with a lot of investors and large scale developers who themselves are looking to cash in on the fast growing population of university undergraduates in towns and cities all over the UK.

Student houses can in many cases be classified as HMOs and it is worth recapping on the previous section to look at whether this type of housing is suitable for your property development and portfolio building strategy.

Like any other house you plan to develop, it will need to conform to current legislation and if the house has multiple occupants, there will need to be adequate soundproofing between the rooms and provision of bathroom and toilet facilities.

Where to find student property

Searching for student property development opportunities is likely to be a long process. You will need to buy in areas of high demand for this kind of property as the further away from University campuses your property is, the less interest there will be. Student's aren't fond of having to commute far to their lectures.

Most of the time the houses that are suitable for conversion into student properties can be found in inner city areas. They are often terraced and it will be obvious from looking around the immediate area that students make up a sizeable proportion of the population.

Who would benefit from investing in student property?

- You have the funds to be able to purchase property close to University Campuses. Prices are usually higher in these areas due to the demand for property and regular supply of tenants.
- You are buying a house for your children to live in while they are at University and then continue letting it to students in the future.
- There is a regular flow of tenants year in year out.

Student Property may not be for you if:

- You don't want to deal with lots of maintenance issues. Houses occupied by students can often end up requiring lots of maintenance and frequent call outs for plumbers and electricians.
- You don't want the extra burden of cleaning up property every 2 to 3 years when your students leave.
- You don't like dealing with the extra paperwork involved when dealing with multiple occupants.

Location is an important factor in any form of property investment but with student property you have the added complication of finding an area where demand is likely to remain high in the long term.

Recent government reforms have hit students hard as well as putting a lid on the rise in international student applications. This will hit some of the lower ranked universities harder than the elite. These trends are worth keeping an eye on to ensure long term success. Check out the Guardian newspaper,s latest university rankings table to see where the best universities are in the country.

Self-Build

If you like to be totally hands on with property development, then you may be considering a self-build. Building a house from scratch is likely to be a lot more difficult and time consuming than developing an existing property.

Self-build is worth considering if you have the funds to do it at scale with multiple properties or on a smaller scale if you want to make better use of land that you own and want to generate additional income from it.

In the latter case, many of the costs associated with self-build can be reduced if you already have detailed knowledge and surveys of the land you own and any planning or environmental restrictions.

If you are considering purchasing land to build your property, then one thing to keep in mind is the type of land. While buying land may seem a straightforward process in comparison to houses, it is vital to buy the right type of land for your building project.

I have known people buy land only to find that their original estimate of building costs was way off the mark because the land they bought had a slope. The costs of getting the land fit for building escalated with the eventual bill coming in at £40,000 more than they had anticipated originally.

The costs of groundwork on sloping sites increase in line with each degree of slope so if the land slopes even by 10 degrees it can add around £10,000 in costs.

So it should come as no surprise that the biggest issues confronting self-build projects are budgeting, motivation and the work involved. Even if you are not hands on, there will still be lots of planning and organisation needed to make sure the project is delivered on time and on budget, or at least as near to your budget as possible.

The upfront costs of self-building are significant and if we go back to our main principles of making money from property, if you invest a lot of money up front to get your project off the ground, it could be years before you make a return.

You may need to prepare yourself for a long wait to get a decent return on investment and most people can ill afford the time it takes to build a house themselves and get it ready for rent or sale.

That said if you find a suitable site or if you already have land set aside, then self- building will not only teach you a lot about the practical side of the property development business, it can also give the experience to tackle larger scale projects as the profits on this type of development can be much higher, particularly when you come to sell.

Auction Property

If you ever find yourself watching daytime TV, you will find plenty of seasoned property investors and developers buying properties at auctions. This is not a route I would personally recommend if you are just starting out as a property developer for a variety of reasons.

Watching people buy property at an auction on TV can be very different to buying yourself. Auctions are often a cauldron of human emotion where the heart can sometimes rule the head. This is when some of the worst mistakes are made.

That said, you can find property that is well below market value at an auction and if the property you find doesn't need a lot of renovation work, you will be paying a lot less for it if you have done your homework beforehand.

One thing you must consider however is why a particular property is being put up for sale at an auction. Anything put up for auction is likely to be sold for less than the owners will have wanted and there is always a reason for this.

Often a property will be a bank repossession, or the original owners might have passed away. The key thing is, whoever wants to sell the property at auction will want to do so quickly.

In this case it is worth doing your research beforehand on how properties are selling in the area where the auction property is located. What is the likely time on the market and how is tenant demand?

Remember Auctions are ideal places to get rid of problems The onus is on the buyer to make sure the property is worth investing in.

Why Can't I just Get A Survey Done?

If you have time before the auction, there is usually nothing to prevent you getting a property surveyed so that you can find out if there are any hidden or expensive problems.

Unfortunately there is just one problem. The survey is going to cost you money whether you manage to buy the property or not unlike a regular purchase when this is done as part of the sale process.

So you will be at an immediate disadvantage if you don't have the skills to spot problems with a building yourself or at least someone who can come along and help you for free.

If you pay for your survey and get outbid at auction, then that money will be lost and you will then be back at square one looking for another property or be under pressure to pay more than you had budgeted for.

What Happens When You Don't Get A Survey Done

With the hassles highlighted above, you may be tempted to simply go ahead, take the risk and hope for the best. There is a chance you might get away with it but then there is also the risk of something bad happening like the true story of an unfortunate investor who decided to buy herself a dream home overlooking the beautiful Devon coastline.

She liked the property so much she placed her bids for the property over the telephone, no doubt gripped by excitement at how fortunate she was to find such a hidden gem.

The property was bought for £154,000, which even in 2010 was cheap for a 6 -bedroom house. The dream lasted for just six days before some rocks at the bottom of the garden fell into the sea.
Then bit by bit, with each passing storm the rest of the garden, before the whole house eventually collapsed down the cliff face never to be seen again.

While this was an extreme case, it does emphasise the need to be cautious and to make sure the heart doesn't rule the head at auctions. Buying at auction with a mortgage

Starting out at as a property developer often means doing so with the help of mortgage finance.

Ultimately, buying at auction can be a risky business because you will need to act quickly to get the mortgage through on time.

Then there is the deposit to find to secure your property. Say for example the property you bid on at auction is sold to you for £100,000. In this case you will need at least £10,000 to put down to secure the property and you will be bound to do so as soon as the hammer falls.

You may have arranged a mortgage prior to auction but if you haven't then you may only have a four weeks to get it arranged or risk losing your deposit if it doesn't!

Further costs might also be incurred while the property is in your possession and you could end up liable for any damage that occurs.

PART TWO:

RENOVATING PROPERTY

Chapter 5

Adding Value

Becoming a property developer goes hand in hand with adding value. It could even be argued that you are adding value to society when you help to tackle the country's housing shortage.

This comes with a certain level of responsibility. This is why becoming a property developer isn't for everyone. Many people will stop at just one property because the very idea of becoming a full-time property developer looks too difficult. It takes a lot of time, effort and cash to do it well.

If you are someone who thrives on doing difficult work and seeing things through, then there is nothing stopping you making a success of property development. Adding value is difficult in any walk of life and not just in property.

Adding value to the properties you develop requires a consideration of where that potential value lies. It will require planning and research to see not only what suits the property but also its location.

For example, there may be little benefit adding an extension or a loft conversion if your target market is young couples living in inner city areas close to the office. It may even be cost prohibitive to make radical structural alterations if the cost outweighs your return on investment.

So adding value starts with making a careful assessment of what buyers or tenants are most likely to want. This will in turn ensure that the time your property is on the market will be reduced.

Developing a property for sale or rent is very different from developing your own home. Adding value to a development property is about getting the basics right first and then adding the parts that are most likely to add appeal for buyers.

At the most basic level, this may mean a fresh coat of paint on the walls, a new kitchen and or bathroom in older properties might also be a good idea.

I see so many rental properties advertised with shabby kitchens and landlords blaming their estate agents for failing to find a tenant. I believe that getting your property in a presentable state will pay off not only in more enquiries but also a better standard of tenant.

Adding value will require some investment on your part and money put by to pay for improvements as and when they are needed. It's easy to fall into the trap of not investing in your property but like any business, lack of investment will come back to bite you someday.

In this chapter we will look at some of the ways you can add value to property, types of improvements that can be made and how to make accurate calculations of how much you should spend (and save) on improvements.

What should be included in a development property?

You will find that developing property doesn't just mean building or refurbishing houses or flats. When the building work is done you will need to satisfy certain buyer or tenant expectations.

What you include in your property will largely depend on the type of buyer or tenant you are aiming to attract, the type of property and whether or not you are preparing a property for sale or to let.

What should be included in a sale property?

This is the easier of the two. Buyers of properties will prefer a blank slate to work with and unless you are developing at scale there is no need to provide a show home.

This doesn't mean you won't need to invest in fixtures, fittings and certain appliances. What you include in a fitted kitchen for example will help increase the appeal of the property.

At the minimum your property should include:

A Cooker
An Oven
A Fridge Freezer
(And ideally a dishwasher and washing machine.)

Buyers will also expect a decent fitted bathroom suite and (or) shower depending on the space you have to work with.

Externally some investment in landscaping is a must to increase the kerb appeal of the property. People will often drive by a house before booking a viewing so it's important not to put them off at this early stage and leave them curious to have a look at what's inside.

Adding a few mature plants to gardens will make the property appear more welcoming but it isn't necessary to go overboard.

What should be included in a rental property?

Some investors new to development make the mistake of furnishing their rental property only to find that it ends up having an impact on their ROI.

While furnishing a property is worthwhile in properties offered to young professionals or students living in the city, it is likely to discourage families or more mature tenants who will prefer to bring their own furniture and sometimes their own appliances as well.

It is also important to consider how much appliances and furniture will cost you long term. The more items you include in a rental property, the more it will cost you in repairs and replacements for those items.

One of the things that quite often goes unnoticed is simple presentation. First impressions are vital whether your property is being offered for sale or for rent, ignoring cleanliness and tidiness will inevitably put buyers off.

People like to feel an instant attraction to somewhere they would like to call home so it's asking a lot for them to use too much of their own imagination.

If appliances etc. are dirty or there are any signs of neglect, then this will do little to attract tenants or at least not the type of tenants you want in your property.

Renovating Listed Buildings

If you are new to property development, then choosing a listed building to renovate will present you with some unique challenges. These challenges will escalate according to how high the grade is.

Listed buildings are classified in three grades:

Grade I : A building of exceptional interest due to its history or importance to the local area.

Grade II*: An important building that is of special interest.

Grade II : Also of special interest but not at the level of importance of those above.

It is unlikely that you will be developing a property with a grade I or grade II * listing which leaves us with some points to cover when it comes to renovating a grade II listed building. 92% of the listed buildings to be found in the UK are grade II listed and as a general rule, the older a building is, the more likely it will be listed.

There are several organisations around the country set up to protect them and other buildings from being harmed by development work. For the most part local authorities will back them up and ignoring certain rules and regulations could land you in hot water and lead to a prison sentence if you're not careful.

So listed buildings are usually chosen by experienced developers equipped to pass strict guidelines and deal with the delays that can often occur when trying to gain approval for certain improvements or modifications.

However, this shouldn't put you off if you know what you are doing. Heritage organisations often encourage sympathetic development if only to help fund the cost of preserving a building. There are even cases where permission has been granted to demolish buildings altogether.

You may even be given access to local authority grants for some projects which can help towards your building costs.

How Do I Find Out If a Building Is Listed?

Finding out what buildings are listed in a particular area is easy. http://www.britishlistedbuildings.co.uk has an extensive list of listed buildings available and you can also find out information from your local authority or heritage groups.

How do I Gain Consent to Renovate a Listed Building?

While you may not need consent to do very minor repairs that replace original features, you may need to apply for consent for more visible alterations and modifications.

Gaining consent can be a time-consuming process with no guarantee of success. Local authorities can take as long as 11 weeks to let you know the outcome of your application and if you fail to convince them, this can mean a lot of wasted weeks.

If you simply carry out the work then apply for permission retrospectively, you run the risk of the application being rejected and this could leave you in trouble and out of pocket when the authorities insist that work needs to be undone.

Depending on how much time you have available, renovating a listed building can be a rewarding experience and you will be helping to preserve the character of the local area. However, this needs to be weighed against what you are aiming to achieve as a property developer in the longer term.

Adding Value – Extensions

With stamp duty now a real issue for anyone buying property for investment, building an extension on an existing property can be a smart way to add value and increase the amount of space available for occupants.

According to some surveys, simply converting a loft can add up to 20% to the value of a property and similar figures are reported for an average-sized extension.

Loft conversions and extensions are particularly popular with property owners in cities where available and affordable land is scarce such as London. Landlords can often add an extra floor if a loft is big enough and in a HMO this can add considerably to rental income.

There is, however, plenty to consider as a developer before you decide to extend a property.

What type of extension is best?

The type of extension you choose will largely depend on any restrictions your property has. If the property has a large enough rear garden then losing some of that outdoor space might be worth it to gain an extra room.

Similarly, if the loft is a decent size and is at least as high as the 7 ft minimum requirement for a bedroom then, converting the loft is likely to pay off even if it can often be one of the most expensive extension options.

Converted lofts create versatile spaces which can add to the appeal of your property from the point of view of tenants and buyers. They can be used for anything from gyms to home offices and even an extra floor if the space is big enough.

The biggest hurdle as I mentioned is likely to be the cost. My builder tells me that a basic conversion will cost from £10,000 (which would be very basic) to around £40,000 if you want to effectively add an extra floor to your property.

An extension is unlikely to cost you less than a loft conversion, so it often boils down to what will suit the property and which will add the most value.

Important things to consider when building an extension

Practical considerations

Once you have decided on the type of extension, it is then important to consider some of the practicalities. Before going any further you should think very carefully about even the smallest extension.

You could even ask yourself is it even necessary or even worth it? Will knocking out a wall be of more benefit?.

One thing that is often overlooked is the availability of parking space. If more people are going to be living in your extended property, then they will usually require more parking spaces.

Even if there is on-street parking outside, you may well find that planning permission is rejected on the basis that there aren't enough parking spaces for additional occupants.

When it comes to the building work itself, is the rear of your property easily accessible or is there no access? Trying to extend the rear of a terraced property could result in a lot of disruption with builders walking in an out of the house with heavy lintels, bricks and so on.

If you are unsure about the suitability of the land around your house, then it is important to find someone who can advise you.

Designing an extension

If you don't have the skills and experience to design and build an extension yourself you will probably need a structural engineer, and or an architect. At the very least you will need someone with the ability to make accurate drawings and plan the layout and structure.

If you want to be certain that this phase goes according to plan it is best to hire someone with the relevant technical qualifications. These people will cost more but they will at least be a member of a recognised organisation such as:

Association of Building Engineers (ABE)
Chartered Institute of Architectural Technologists (CIAT)
Chartered Institute of Building (IOB)
Institution of Structural Engineers (ISE)
Royal Institution of Chartered Surveyors (RICS)

It is important to bear in mind that hiring a qualified architect or structural engineer will be considerably more expensive. The cost can sometimes outweigh the benefits with smaller extensions.

Finding a Builder

Again finding a good builder should ensure that your extension project is delivered on time and on budget. I always advise going with someone who has worked on similar projects before and comes with a recommendation from someone you know well.

Make sure that the quote you receive is accurate, binding and not subject to significant add-ons and make sure that everything is included. I often hear stories of builders saying that certain tasks are not included in the price.

Also estimates can vary widely so it is wise to get at least 3 quotes to compare. If one quote is considerably lower than the others it may be worth finding out why.

If you are a first time property developer, building an extension can be a great introduction to what it takes to make the best of a property and add value. The practical experience and planning involved may also provide you with valuable skills you can use in further projects.

Chapter 6

Self Building & Developing For Profit

You might see lots of people on TV shows like Grand Designs building amazing homes for themselves but the proportion of people who actually self-build in the UK is actually extremely low.

According to one recent survey, the number of people who decided to take matters into their own hands and build themselves a house was just 8% of UK homes in a 12- month period.

I suspect that the number of these people building houses to sell on or let for profit was substantially lower even than this.

So it seems that despite the appeal of managing one's own house building project from start to finish, few people in the UK will actually go through with it, so there has to be something that puts people off.

This something often relates to the costs involved. The biggest hurdle is the high cost of building materials and of course buying plots of land, gaining planning permission and the time involved.

Is it possible to self-build and make a profit?

For anyone hoping to make money as a property developer, this is the most important question to answer. Self-build projects can be a huge task to take on even for people who have some of the important practical skills.

I have known experienced builders embark on a self-build project only to find the cost of the project far outweighed what they might have made from it in the short term.

Cost of Building A Basic 3 Bedroom House (Source: Land Registry)

Cost to do it yourself

£85,000

Average cost of hiring tradespeople to do it for you

£150,000

Buying a new build house

£200,000

The cost involved in building a basic three-bedroom house yourself without any help from skilled tradespeople will come in at approximately £85,000 which is a significant saving on a buying a house which would come in at an average £200,000 depending on where you live.

Hire a team of tradespeople to build the house for you and the price rises significantly to £150,000.

You may then need to factor in costs for improving local infrastructure. Building a property from scratch often means extra costs in this area people didn't necessarily expect when starting out.

So if you are considering a self-build you not only need to factor in the time involved, which can be more than a year depending on how much time you have available, you will also need to do a careful estimate of how much profit you are likely to make.

Making a profit in the short term is unlikely given the upfront costs and time involved and it is only when houses are built in volume that these costs can then be outweighed by the profits generated from selling those properties.

Another way to generate more profit from self-build is to turn a property into flats to multiply the return on rents. A lot will depend on what part of the country you intend to build your property and local market demand which we will cover in the next section.

What does the local market need?

If you can take a step back for a moment and look at property development as a business, the fundamental part of the success of that business is to establish what your market needs.

So the first stage of establishing what the local market needs is to do your research. This research will begin with the kind of people who will be buying or renting your property and how your property will meet their requirements.

You must then look at the size of that market. If you are building or developing a property to fulfil the needs of a particular type of purchaser or tenant, then there needs to be enough of them to ensure that you are not struggling to make a sale or find suitable tenants.

While assessing need in a local market isn't an exact science, doing some thorough research will at least give you some indications of where demand lies.

As a general rule there will be areas where demand is high for family housing because there is a school with a good rating from Ofsted, Estyn (Wales) or (Education Scotland) depending on where the property is located.

Parents are particularly keen on the whole to send their children to good primary and secondary schools and it follows that houses in these areas will be worth more than their equivalents in areas where schools are not up to standard.

If you are developing flats or HMOs then these will usually be in areas of high employment such as city and town centres, or close to industrial estates and retail parks.

If you are developing properties to let to students, then it will need to be reasonably close to the campus of a popular university.

Why local demand isn't always constant

While you can reasonably expect demand for property to remain high in some locations, there will be some areas where demand for property will depend on economic and even political factors.

Brexit is an example of a seismic movement in the political landscape which can transform lives either for better or for worse.

One of the biggest drivers for demand in some localised property markets is the influx of people moving in from Europe to find work. A large proportion will seek work in factories and areas where demand for labour is high.

So it follows that demand for accommodation will rise in tandem with the amount of jobs created.

If this freedom of movement is somehow restricted or if there is an economic downturn severe enough to close down the businesses that employ not only immigrant workers but also local people, then it is likely those people will begin to move elsewhere to find work. This will then lead to a significant drop in demand for housing.

So if you are planning to buy property in areas where demand depends on more specific or transient economic and political factors, then this will carry its own risks if you are then left with a property that fails to generate an income.

Beyond this we live in an age where data and information is freely available on the Internet. It is easy to for example to find out how long properties are on the market simply by looking at Rightmove. Similarly, you can see historical information on sale prices which can give you a pretty good idea of the level of demand over time.

If the Internet isn't your thing, then the next most obvious place to go is your estate agent, who will be able to give you their advice on the best locations to help you make an informed decision.

Your Rights To Build

From a builder in Harlow who had to have his development demolished because he didn't seek planning permission to the famous actress Anna Friel who was told to rebuild or demolish an extension on her house in Windsor - becoming a victim of local planning laws can happen to anyone.

Even if planning is approved by the local authority as was the case with Anna Friel, there may be certain rules to follow which must be understood by builders contractors or yourself if you are doing the work by yourself.

Issues often relate to preserving the character of areas, so if anything is deemed unsightly or likely to impact on other residents in the area in some way, planning issues can soon have a costly impact on your plans.

Assuming you have done your homework on local planning, then gaining permission should be relatively straightforward particularly now the government is keen to encourage more people to self-build to help increase the supply of affordable homes.

This provides an unprecedented opportunity for those who do have the resources to self-build to do so with support from local authorities.

In fact a new scheme has only just come into force aimed at doing just that. It is called Right to Build. What this means in essence is that local authorities are required to release and make more plots available for people who want to build a home themselves.

A portal has been set up by National Custom and Self Build Association, where people can register their interest called the Right To Build Portal http://www.righttobuildportal.org/.

At the time of writing the scheme is only available in England but there are plans in place that could mean that it is rolled out into Scotland and Wales.

As part of the registration process, you will be asked to apply as an individual or as part of a group and the kinds of plots you will have access to will largely depend on whether you are opting for a rural or urban plot.

The latter is likely to consist mainly of brownfield plots suitable for flats while the former may mean compromising on having your own plot with acres of land it.

The main reasons individuals have been put off by self-building have been access to finance, access to plots and planning regulations.

While there is still some way to go to improve the finance side of things (there are still relatively few products aimed at self-builders), Right to Build should at least address the problems of availability of land and some of the restrictions that have made life difficult for people starting out.

8 Amateur Developer Mistakes To Avoid

When you start out as a property developer it is easy to make mistakes. The worst mistake of all is to spend more money than you are making.

If you find that building work is starting to eat into your finances to the point where you are having to borrow and put money on credit cards just to get by, then as my grandmother would say, you are living beyond your means.

Maintaining a realistic budget is, as we established earlier, an essential part of becoming a successful property developer.

Aside from being reckless with finances here are some of the other mistakes made by property developers starting out.

1. Developing property in the wrong part of the country

Failing to heed the advice of doing research on a local market and then investing in the wrong location will not only kill your cashflow, it can leave you significantly out of pocket.

Lots of people dream of finding that next up and coming area and making killing on buying a property cheap, but property is usually cheap for a reason - few people want to live there.

I often hear of companies attempting to sell buy to let properties in the U.S. city of Detroit. You can buy a house there for $25,000 but with high crime rates and low employment why would you? It may have been a thriving industrial hub filled with blue collar car workers once, but those days are long gone.

There are locations in the UK with similar problems, the many coal mines and car plants that once sustained whole towns and villages have long since closed for good. While some of these locations can be revived with a bit of investment and re-invention, there will be plenty more that never seem to recover.

2. Going overboard on finance

Lending terms for buy to let are not as generous as they are for residential property. Even less so if you happen to be building your property from scratch. One of the biggest pitfalls in property investment is borrowing money and not being able to afford the repayments on the loan.

To avoid this, it is worth shopping around for better deals. It is also wise to be realistic about how much money you will need to fund the project from the start through to completion. Underestimating this can leave you having to find cash from your savings as costs escalate.

3. Getting Conned By The Builder

I have to say that 90% of the builders and tradespeople you deal with will be honest with their quotes. Unfortunately, there will always be a small minority who take advantage.

Common problems include works taking much longer than anticipated followed by additional costs that were not discussed at the beginning of a project. To avoid this, make sure you get a fixed quote for the work from the beginning rather than an estimate.

Sadly, there isn't much you can do if you haven't made some important agreements on timeframes and cost from the outset.

4. Economising on the things that matter

Depending on the kind of market you are aiming at for your property, it is always worth spending as much as you can afford on the items that matter. This includes flooring and kitchen fittings as well as the materials you use on the outside.

If you cut corners on these areas and buy faux versions, potential buyers will notice and if you intend to put the property on the market to let, over time cheaper fixtures and fitting probably won't last as long and you will then have the added cost further down the line of replacing them. The same goes for any appliances.

5. Spending too much on fixtures and fittings

While we have established that it is best not to buy cheap, the same thing could also be said for buying expensive. You have got to separate yourself from the equation when developing property and keep things simple.

Splashing out on marble bathrooms and granite worktops may work for more exclusive buyers but it is unlikely you will be able to command a higher price for your property just because you spend more money on the interior.

6. Too many small rooms

This one is more likely to affect developers who build a property from scratch. The belief is that the more bedrooms a property has the more it will be worth. This can be true of course if there is room for the extra rooms and enough space for people to feel comfortable.

I once met an estate agent who told me that a bedroom was perfectly adequate because there was just enough room to squeeze in a small airbed.

Don't make this mistake with your property. It is better to have three good sized bedrooms than 4 tiny bedrooms.

7. Rushing the work

If you find yourself rushing to complete work or rushing into a project without adequate planning beforehand, then this puts you at greater risk of messing up your development project or not adhering to local planning regulations. Make sure you spend time completing all the necessary paperwork and give yourself enough time to do the work properly. This will certainly pay off in the end even if you find yourself itching to get started.

8. Being too greedy

It's hard to succeed at anything in the long term if you are greedy. Things are no different if you are a property developer. It is ok to be greedy buying property if you can afford it, but don't price the property you sell too high just because you think it is better than others in the area. Buyers are savvy about what houses are worth nowadays and you don't want your property to be sitting on the market for months.

Should You Hire A Project Manager?

Developing property for the first time can be a daunting prospect. So it is only natural to look for help in dealing with all the various tasks you will be faced with during the project.

These tasks can range from the day to day planning and management of the development project to managing budgets, safety and contractors. All of the things that you really should be working on if you want to gain the experience necessary to succeed.

In fact, if you are looking for a project manager to work on a small scale project, you are likely to be disappointed. You will find it hard to find anyone willing to commit the time unless you are developing at scale and in case if you are hiring a builder, they should have the necessary skills to manage projects themselves.

Even if you do find someone willing to handle your project, handing over too much control of budgets and spending additional funds on a project manager will have a further unnecessary impact on your bottom line.

Where project managers are worth the investment is in projects involving several contractors and multiple properties. Coordinating everything so that the process runs smoothly is where the real value in project management lies.

Project managers can work right from the beginning of the project with architects to oversee designs and amendments to plans and layouts and solve any problems that may arise during the project.

A project manager is likely to be working on site every day to ensure that deliverables are being met and knowledge is transferred between the various parties involved from architects to builders and other contractors.

Producing regular feedback is also an important part of a project managers duties and this will help ensure that progress is made and the work is likely to be completed faster as a result.

While hiring a project manager is not usually a requirement for a property developer starting out, you will need to acquire some of the skills and keep a close eye on how things are progressing to make sure deadlines are met and work is carried out according to the specifications.

Design, layout and floor plans

If you are planning the layout of your development, then there are some important rules to keep in mind to ensure that you are building a property that will appeal to the type of buyer or tenant you have in mind. A good floor plan is a critical part of this.

Ensure that the floor plan is flexible

Floor plans need to be carefully considered and require a certain amount of imagination. You will need to imagine how people will move around the home and use the space in each room.

Your tenants or potential buyers may demand more or less of a property depending on where it is located. Over time how people use various spaces changes and you will need to be mindful of this when creating floor plans.

Open plan spaces tend to have more appeal than lots of individual rooms with partitions however the latter might be better if a house is being converted into a HMO or student property where there will be a need for privacy.

Designing layouts your market demands

Some of the latest innovations in property layouts include the super mews houses that are springing up in London with price tags of £6 million. This style of housing combines the convenience of apartments and the charm of traditional mews style housing.

While this is at the more expensive end of property development, it shows how layouts can be adapted to suit particular types of buyers. In expensive areas of London, the super mews is one way to maximise the space available in a way that will appeal to wealthy buyers and tenants who want to live in areas with the most prestigious postcodes.

What Makes A Good Floor Plan?

One of the things we touched on earlier was flexibility of space. At the heart of a good floor plan is a nice flow between the spaces.

A good floorplan will also have enough flexibility to appeal to a wide cross section of buyers or potential tenants. For example if you are thinking of a room as a child's bedroom, it should also be versatile enough to be turned into an office. This will require some thought as to where sockets are located and the amount of natural light that is entering the room.

A kitchen shouldn't be too far from where guests are seated and increasingly these days people prefer their kitchens to be part of a larger dining and entertaining space in smaller homes.

It is also important to look at insulating rooms from general noise and to provide limit the costs of heating various spaces. Floor to ceiling windows might look great on your plans, but if they are going to mean extra heating costs or the incorporation of extra radiators, they may not be an ideal solution.

Finally the most important thing about floor plans is to have one. According to a recent Rightmove study buyers rated floor plans a top priority. One in five people would actually ignore a property that didn't have a floorplan attached. Moreover, floorplans were rated more important than pictures or descriptions!

Getting Out – Selling Your Property

While it is always better to try and hang on to your investment until you are sure of making at least a modest profit, a change in circumstances can often change in the time it takes to renovate or build a property and this can lead to you needing to sell quickly to avoid further costs or to pay back finances.

If you find yourself in this position don't worry, you are certainly not alone. You will find plenty of development projects that have been abandoned when property owners have overstretched themselves or underestimated how much money they needed to complete work.

If you do find yourself in this position then there are fortunately some ways to help yourself out of a potentially sticky situation and sell your property faster.

Selling with planning permission

Sometimes selling property can be difficult, particularly when markets are sluggish due to the time of year, or an economic downturn. One way to add value and get the price you want is to sell with planning permission.

Planning permission for various improvements can add value to your property particularly when those improvements will add a significant amount of value. You may be able to add as much as 10% to the value of property if permission is granted for an extension, basement or perhaps a loft conversion. The biggest benefit of all is being able to sell your property faster with it than without it.

Even better it is likely you will already have gained planning permission as part of your development plans from the start so if you do have a change of fortunes or decide that the cost is too much you can at least hope for a quick sale.

What Improvements should you include in your application for planning permission?

Fashions change in housing just as much as anywhere else and at present loft conversions are making a big comeback. A completed loft conversion can add up to 20% to the value of your property, so selling your property with permission for a loft conversion will probably attract plenty of interest from buyers and other property developers. The same can be said for permission to extend property.

Conservatories also remain popular and will likely be more appealing in terms of potential when it comes to cost compared to loft conversions and extensions.

Often conservatories will fall into permitted development depending on your location but it is always best to check if this is the case.

With the stamp duty increases that came in recently for those investing in second properties, having planning permission to extend existing properties and getting around extra taxes can be particularly appealing for some buyers who can save money on their purchase and add value to the property later on.

How Much Will It Cost To Gain Planning Permission?

Planning permission is likely to cost in the region of £400 and this is in addition to architect fees. Once you have submitted your plans for approval it can take up to 12 weeks to get a decision. The cost and time involved in gaining planning permission could just be more than covered by getting a quick sale and achieving the asking price.

Tax issues to be aware of when selling

The biggest impact to your finances, if you are planning to sell your investment property in the future, could be a monster tax bill in the form of capital gains (CGT).

There are two rates of capital gains tax depending on your income. The standard rate is 18% and the higher rate currently stands at 28%.

If you happen to fall in to the higher bracket, then the CGT you pay could be several thousand pounds more than under the old rules.

How Is CGT on Investment Property Calculated?

CGT is payable on the increase in value of your asset while you own it with certain exceptions. If you have lived in the property for a certain length of time, then amount you are required to pay will be discounted. This is called apportionment.

The amount of CGT you pay will also depend on your overall income including that from employment or your business. So there will be cases where the amount of profit you make on a property sale plus what you earn puts you over the £42,385 threshold which will mean CGT is payable at 28% rather than the 18% you will be liable for if your income comes in under this amount.

For example:

Income from employment: £20,000

Taxable Gain: £10,000
Annual Allowance: 11,100
Tax rate 18%

Income from employment: £35,000

Taxable Gain: £25,000
Annual Allowance: 11,100
£7,385 (taxable 18%)
Amount remaining over £42,385 (taxable at 28%)

Fortunately there are ways to reduce this tax bill. One is to transfer a share of the property to your spouse and benefit from their CGT allowance. This will only work if they don't have their own CGT liability of course!

Another way to pay less tax is to make a contribution to your pension in the form of a lump sum. You will presently receive tax relief on contributions up to £40,000 a year. There are other methods including investing in start-up businesses, however these put your money at risk if those businesses subsequently fail to take off and you don't recoup the money on your investment.

For further advise on this tailored to your own particular requirements, it is worth consulting an expert.

Chapter 7

Working on Site Yourself

When I started out, I found the practical side of property development extremely rewarding and I managed to acquire many skills that have helped me since.

In this chapter I will be introducing you to some of the ways you can improve your practical skills as well as introduce you to some of the realities you will face when working on site.

Before you consider working on the practical side of property development yourself, if you don't have experience it is very important to ensure your own safety and that of others. Make sure you are covered by insurance and that you are familiar with health and safety rules and regulations. Construction sites can be dangerous places to work and even more so for people without experience.

How to improve your practical DIY and Building skills

Getting stuck in with the practical side of property development isn't for everyone and even for those who do want to have a go, it can be a daunting prospect.

I'm a firm believer that you can acquire any skill if you put your mind to it and have the will to succeed. It is certainly achievable for anyone to acquire skills in bricklaying plastering plumbing and even electrical work if you are prepared to do some training. Admittedly it takes five years to qualify as an electrician and practical experience so this may not be the best place to start.

While it is unlikely you will want to try and acquire all the above skills at once assuming you don't have experience in them already, there is nothing wrong with having a go and you may even save a fortune hiring contractors to do the work for you. This will certainly help if you are planning to expand your property portfolio by developing properties in need of attention.

Back in the old days there was little option other than to buy a book, shadow a professional or try and learn from experience. Today there is no shortage of help available and the best starting point has to be online.

If I need to see how something is done I simply search on YouTube and there will be thousands of experts demonstrating how to do it.

While books are useful in describing the basics, videos can help a lot because you get to see someone actually doing what is described.

If you would rather get out and about and learn practical DIY skills from others, then your friends or family can be the best place to start.

Most families have at least one member who is good at something related to building work. The caveat here is that the handy person isn't teaching you bad habits.

Finally hiring a contractor to start the work for you can mean you acquire the skills you need simply by watching them and helping out. Not all of your contractors will appreciate this however and would rather have you pay them to do the whole job than rectify any problems that may arise from doing the work yourself.

When it comes to multiple properties you will need to assess how much time you have to get involved in practical work. As with running a business, there is probably more money to be made employing contractors to do the work for you rather than do all the heavy lifting yourself.

Getting help – Hiring good tradespeople

Good tradespeople are worth their weight in gold. You may already know some people who can do some of the more skilled property development work for you but if you don't then you need to be careful about who you hire.

Most people will go by recommendations when choosing a builder, electrician, plumber and so on. However just because they may have worked on a friend's kitchen or they have done some basic electrical work at their house, this doesn't always guarantee that they will be a good fit for your project.

Some of these recommended builders might not have a landline or a website and I would recommend that you avoid anyone who doesn't have a landline, website or other point of reference.

Ideally the tradespeople you work with should have experience on jobs similar to what you are asking them to do. If possible it is a good idea to go and see what they have done for others rather than trust a recommendation alone.

Then, it is always good to get at least three quotes for the jobs you are asking them to do and make sure you are providing them with as much detail as possible. This means you will get a more accurate quote from everyone as failing to provide them with full details can mean paying more than you have budgeted for.

You will find that some people advise that you don't pay your tradesperson in advance, but this really depends on the scope of the project. It reasonable for a builder to ask for a deposit before starting work to cover any material costs and so on.

If you are handing over cash, make sure you have something in writing which gives a clear summary of the work that will be carried out and what is expected from both parties.

Using The Internet To Find A Tradesperson

Over the years a variety of websites have sprung up to fill the 'find a trader niche' and some are better than others. Trustatrader.com Ratedpeople and consumer website Which are just some examples.

When using the Internet it has to be remembered that you can't trust anything commercial 100%. You don't need to be a master with computers to fake a review for your friends if they happen to be promoting their services on some websites.

If you are choosing your tradespeople online, be wary and try to go on government and other not-for-profit websites to source the people you need.

Key safety issues to be aware of when working on site

Whether you are actively involved in the building and construction work on your property or you are simply helping out, building sites are hazardous places.

The constant changing nature of a construction sites is the main reason why the industry is one of the most dangerous places to work in despite some major advances in health and safety over the years.

If you are hiring contractors then they will no doubt bring with them experience and knowledge of health and safety procedures and rules. If you are working on site with them, then it is important to familiarise yourself with these rules to prevent not only injury to yourself but also to others working on site.

Some of the biggest risks on a construction site involve taking short cuts or cutting corners on particular jobs and there are plenty of others to consider depending on how much work is required on particular property developments including:

Moving equipment and materials

Construction sites are dynamic environments where people machinery and vehicles are all moving around at once. It is important that any work that involves moving materials or lifting heavy objects is done well away from individuals who are working nearby.

Working at height

One of the most hazardous areas of construction work involves working at height. Many accidents involve people falling from heights on building sites whether as part of demolition or construction work. Proper health and safety training is essential for those operating cranes and other equipment and great care must be taken to reduce other risks associated with working high above ground level.

Noise from equipment and machinery

Noise on a construction site can be an issue if you don't wear ear protection. Most damage to hearing comes from excessive exposure to repetitive noise over a length of time. If you are hiring a construction company to work on your development then they should have the correct procedures in place to remove any risk of damage to hearing.

Slips, Trips and Falls

With materials constantly being moved around a construction site, some of the biggest risks involve trips and falls. It is impossible to eliminate all the risks but ensuring that a construction site is kept as tidy as possible should reduce the chances of tripping over materials or falling into holes in the ground.

Manual Handling

Working in construction involves lots of lifting and manoeuvring so there is a risk of injury particularly to the back which takes a lot of the strain when lifting. Again there should be set procedures and rules about how much weight can be lifted safely on site and the correct posture to use.

Asbestos

While Asbestos is unlikely to be a problem in newer properties, older properties may well contain asbestos which is harmful when it is disturbed. Inhaling the fibres can lead to fatal diseases involving the lungs so it is important to establish if asbestos is present in a building. If it is then it will require specialist removal.

Sourcing materials

Depending on the scale of the project and whether or not you will be doing some or all of the work yourself you may be faced with the dilemma of where to source materials.

As with most things concerning property development, a lot will depend on your budget. The cost of materials can escalate quickly and even the smallest orders can soon add up.

Material and labour costs will certainly make up the lion's share of what you will be spending and this will inevitably eat into your profits even if you may be able to claim some back on tax.

With development projects ranging from minor refurbishment to self-builds the route you go to source materials will also depend how much material you need. For smaller projects, it is easier to source materials yourself.

You will find there are plenty of local suppliers who can provide just about anything you are likely to need for your development. For large scale projects, it is easier to use a builder's merchant.

If they are local, they should be able to offer in-depth knowledge of local materials as well as advice on quantities and lead times if you bring detailed plans along. If you open up a trade account you should receive a generous discount on usual prices.

Rather than using a merchant, you could choose to go it alone and source your materials without the middle man. This is only really an option for experienced builders or someone prepared to work full time doing it.

Buying Your Materials From Reclamation Yards

If sustainability is important to you, then sourcing materials from reclamation or salvage yards is an ideal way to reduce impact on the environment.

The construction industry in general is under pressure to become more sustainable. The scale of waste and pollution produced by the manufacturing of construction materials accounts for a third of waste material in the UK and 18% of carbon dioxide emissions.

Much of the pollution comes from transportation of construction materials as well as the manufacturing process. If materials are sourced from abroad then the carbon footprint and impact on the environment is considerably higher.

If you are considering using reclaimed materials for your building project, then you are likely to be part of a small minority. Currently just 1% of building projects make use of reclaimed materials. This is partly due to the difficulty in finding enough materials to complete larger construction projects.

If the property you are developing is listed or a period property then reclamation yards are certainly worth a look. You will find all sorts of reclaimed building materials and various architectural features which can be used to add character to a property.

Items such as reclaimed slate can save you money on having to buy new slate tiles for a roof project and you will generally save money on other materials too. Historic buildings are being demolished all the time to make way for development. Buying reclaimed is a way to not only preserve this material but also add a touch of character and quality to your building project.

Useful websites

You will find there is a website for just about anything today and that includes all aspects of developing property for sale or let. Here are a selection of some of the most useful.

homebuilding.co.uk

The next best thing to buying the magazine in print is to visit their website. Here you will find a comprehensive archive of articles written on various subjects concerned with property. From self builds to home improvements, everything is covered on the practical side.

self-build.co.uk

This is the online presence of popular construction magazine Built It. You will find plenty of expert advice and articles covering everything you need to know about building. You will also find many of the features inspiring.

which.co.uk

Which has been around for a long time helping out consumers and the website remains a great place to go for advice and ratings. You can search in all parts of the country for trusted traders to help with your development project.

landlords.org.uk

You will find plenty of websites offering advice to landlords and investors. Landlords.org is impartial and full of advice and resources to help you with all the issues that might affect you as a landlord.

architecture.com

Home of the Royal Institute of British Architects RIBA, you can find pretty much everything you need to know about architecture. This includes where to find architects that are members of RIBA, associated services and possibly inspiration for your own project.

ribabookshops.com

This website showcases the latest books on architecture, planning and so on. You can order any books that may be of use to you direct from the website.

www.gov.uk

If you want to find out about any laws, rules and regulations that might have an impact on your development project then this is a good place to start. The government website will give you information on anything from green initiatives to your responsibility as a landlord.

citizenadvice.org.uk

The Citizens Advice website can help with information on various legal issues you might encounter. It also offers advice to tenants which may be useful for landlords to know.

barbourproductsearch.info

Barbour Product Search is a website which connects customers with construction materials suppliers. Using this website and others like it can help save you time searching for various suppliers.

nickfox.co.uk

If you want to know the secrets to making money from property and developing a million pound property portfolio, then visit my own website where you will find stacks of information on anything from HMOs to home study courses.

PART THREE:

PREPARING YOUR PROPERTY

Chapter 8

Applying the Finishing Touches

No doubt it has been a quite journey to get this far. Like any long project it's always a great feeling to finally be nearing completion and even better to be proud that you have achieved something special.

You can now count yourself among a select group of people who have either built or refurbished and transformed a property into a money-making asset.

What happens now?

While adding the final finishing touches and preparing your property for sale or rent isn't going to be anything like as hard as the work you have being doing to get this far, there are still some important areas to consider which will ensure that you not only get the best returns for your property but also comply with various rules and regulations, particularly as far as tenants are concerned.

You will also be faced with some decisions over what is to be included in your property and how much design input is needed. While you may not be providing a show home for potential buyers or tenants, the amount of finishing work required will depend a lot on location and the type of property. It is also important to make sure that you keep within your budget, even though there is likely to be a lot to do to get your property ready for tenants or viewings from potential buyers.

Some of the additional fees you will need to pay before putting your property on the market include:

- Monthly mortgage repayments
- Contingency money
- Costs related to meeting regulatory safety standards
- Purchasing of furniture, appliances and any other equipment
- Legal fees
- Letting agent and management fees (if required)
- Insurance

How Preparing A Home For Let Differs From Preparing A Home For Sale

Preparing a property for let is considerably more complicated than preparing a property for sale. When someone purchases a property, they will have a survey carried out and make the decision to buy based on its findings.

A new property will also be sold with only the bare minimum of fixtures and fittings in place. Preparing a home for let on the other hand will mean including everything required to make the property habitable, although not necessarily furniture.

If you are letting your property furnished, you will need to ensure that it meets minimum safety standards and if you want to attract good tenants to a furnished property, then good tenants will expect good quality furniture.

You should already have in mind your target market and as a general rule, the longer your tenant stays in the property the less you are likely to spend preparing a property every time there is a change of tenant.

Interior design doing it yourself vs hiring a professional

In most cases when starting out as a property developer it is unlikely you will require the services of an interior designer but this depends on many things – if the property is for sale or let, how much time you have at your disposal, and the type of market you are aiming at.

Larger developers will appoint interior designers to work on show homes to attract buyers. Interior designers will also work on large scale developments where apartments are sold to investors fully furnished or with furniture packs so that they can be brought to market and let quickly. These apartments are usually in city centres where there are a high number of young professionals living and working.

If you are simply developing a property for sale it is unlikely you will be doing this in the city centre given the cost of acquiring property and land. Property buyers usually prefer a blank slate to put their own stamp on things.

If you do plan to be letting your property furnished and again you don't have the necessary interior design skills to make it look good, then hiring a professional can be a good investment. As any experienced property investor will tell you – anything that improves your chances of attracting the right kind of tenant is a good investment.

What Does An Interior Designer Do?

If you are hiring an interior designer then it is worth finding out if they have the right level of qualifications for what you are asking them to do. Interior design might look easy and many people fancy themselves as amateur interior designers without understanding what is involved in doing it properly.

Qualifications for interior design range from diplomas to degrees and like any other design discipline, you need to have a good understanding of what it takes to transform an interior from a blank canvas into the kind of interior that will have tenants queuing up.

A qualified interior designer can deal with everything inside including layouts, lighting furniture, furnishings and even architectural elements depending on how big the project is. In addition to this they will remove the headache of sourcing furniture and materials and take on project management where this is required.

Let's face it most of us lack even basic interior design skills so if your property needs to stand out in a competitive rental market, then hiring an interior designer may be worth it.

Doing it yourself can be time consuming. Shopping for equipment and materials and getting everything for the right price can be difficult and time consuming. There may also need to be further preparations needed and work to be organised for delivery which in itself can delay completion with days adding up to weeks on some projects.

Beware however that hiring an interior designer with the right qualifications can be expensive with prices ranging from £25 an hour to several hundred. If your designer is involved in the project for a length of time then these costs can really add up.

7 things to remember when presenting your property for sale

As the old saying goes first impressions last and this is particularly true about property. You may hear some buyers say they have a feeling about a house, but that feeling is only likely to be there if enough attention has been on presentation.

Selling a house you have just built or completely refurbished will be completely different to selling a house you may be living in. One of the obvious advantages of not living in the property is being able to keep the slate blank so that buyers can make up their own minds without it being clouded by other people's tastes in furniture, décor and so on.

That said there are still some things to remember to ensure that you are presenting your property in a way that will get you a quick sale.

1. Get rid of clutter

One of the worst mistakes made when presenting a house for sale is to leave it cluttered. Make sure all tools, paint tins, ladders and so on are removed from the property. Also clean up any mess left behind during rebuilding or refurbishment so that your potential buyer is not put off. It can be incredibly off-putting even if you are interested to have your view obscured and it can also make a property appear smaller than it actually is.

2. Keep paint colours neutral

If you are painting the walls of your property, it is always best to stick to neutral colours. If you are fitting carpets, then they should also be in neutral colours to maintain a clean spacious appearance. A buyer will want to see themselves in a property which means avoiding the introduction of your own preferences.

3. Give it a deep clean

It is always wise to deep clean a property before presenting it to buyers. Buyers won't want to see evidence of the building work that has taken place and will expect all rooms to be presented ready to decorate with no dust or rubble lying around. Windows should be cleaned. All the main building jobs should already be finished in any case before making the property available for viewings

4. Take care of the outside

If you are presenting a house for sale which has a garden and other outdoor space, there is no harm in adding a few plants and doing a bit of landscaping work to increase the kerb appeal of the property. While it isn't worth going overboard, buyers will find a property more attractive if a property is clean and tidy on the outside.

5. Show off the best features

While your property may be empty, this shouldn't stop you from drawing attention to the architectural features of the house. If it's a period property people will want to see those period features.

6. Allow ventilation

Open doors and windows before people arrive for viewings to ensure that you get rid of stale air and any empty house smells. Plugging in some air fresheners might also be a good idea.

7. Be present but not too visible

If you are going to be showing people around the property rather than an agent, be careful not to crowd them out. Allow them to take some time to explore the property themselves and make their own minds up.

PART FOUR:

MAKING MONEY FROM PROPERTY DEVELOPMENT

Chapter 9

Managing Property for Profit

How To Calculate Your Rental Yield

The most important thing to learn if you are to achieve big things in property development is how to calculate net rental yield. Remember you are in it for the money, so it's important the financials stack up.

To help us understand how a net rental yield is calculated, let's use the example of William a typical buy to let investor:

William is looking for property that will earn him a good return on his investment over time. He looks at all the available options and settles on two for comparison.

- The first property is valued at £130,000 with a potential rental return of £600 a month
- The second property is valued at £200,000 with a rental return of £850 a month

Which property should he invest in? Should he invest in the first property which will have lower upfront costs and mortgage payments or should he go for option two, which offers and £250 a month in rental income?

This is where calculating the yield will help William decide which offers the best investment.

The basic formula used for calculating the gross rental yield (this is an important distinction we will return to later) is as follows:

MRR = monthly rental return

I = investment

Yield = MRR x12/I x100

This means William's rental yield for the first property would be:

Monthly rental return = £600

Investment = £130,000

£600 x 12 = £7,200

£7,200 / £130,000 = 0.0553

0.0553 x 100 = 5.54 % yield

His rental yield for the second property would be:

Monthly rental return = £850

Investment = £200,000

£600 * 12 = £10,200

£10,200 / £200,000 = 0.051

0.051 x 100 = 5.1 % yield

So despite the rental income being higher, the yield falls short of that achieved by the cheaper property.

So looking purely at a simple calculation of the yields on both properties, William will be better off investing in the cheaper property because the yield on that property is higher.

Now this kind of yield is not far off the average in many UK cities, however this basic calculation still won't give William enough information to make a final investment decision. To make that decision he will need to look at several variables and factor in costs such as:

- Advertising the property
- Insurance
- Mortgage costs
- Solicitor fees
- Survey fees
- Ongoing costs of redecorating/maintenance
- Running costs during void periods
- Costs of furniture and white goods

Deducting these costs will give a truer picture of the actual return on investment from the property referred to as the 'Net' yield. If you can deduct these costs from your gross yield and still achieve a yield of more than 5%, this will be a good return on investment.

Another point to consider is that rents will inevitably rise over time. This will only increase your likely yield and there is also capital growth to consider. The value of the property itself should also rise over time, assuming you invest well

The Best Locations in the UK for Yields

The best locations for rental returns can be found mainly outside of London and the South East. This is due to property being more expensive to purchase in the south compared to the north which impacts significantly on yields.

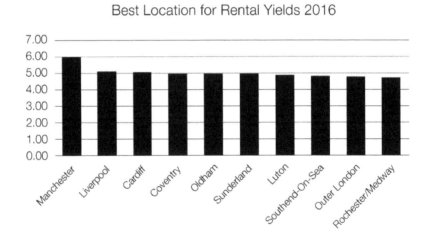

Best Location for Rental Yields 2016

Source: www.simplybusiness.co.uk, 2016

The Best Locations For Capital Growth

If you are looking purely for capital growth potential, then inner London is a clear leader. This is great if your budget stretches to purchasing property in the capital and the South East.

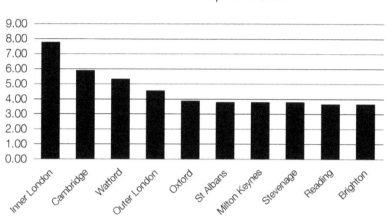

Best Location for Capital Growth

Source: www.simplybusiness.co.uk, 2016

How much rent should you charge

Charging the right amount of rent is fundamental to your success if you are developing property for letting purposes. Charge the wrong amount of rent and you will either end up out of pocket at the end of each month or potential tenants will be put off if they feel the rent is too high compared to other properties in the area – even if those properties seem inferior.

If you have followed the process outlined in this book, you will have already done your research and have an understanding of the local market and what your home is worth, which is the first step in setting the rent.

Depending on how hands-on you want to be when advertising your property, it is probably a wise option to get an agent to come up with a monthly rental figure that will attract enquiries. Rather than trust your agent's judgement entirely, also do some research yourself. Rightmove and Zoopla will have properties advertised similar to yours, so this automatically provides you with some valuable data on the local market.

The average rent charged in the UK as of 2016 is £902pcm according to Homelet which marked a 3% increase on 2015. Look deeper into rental statistics and you will find significant regional variations ranging from £1542pcm in London to £525pcm in the North East, which is more than two thirds lower.

It is also important to note that rental markets can be volatile and change month to month. If your property is going on the market in the autumn and winter months, you might struggle to let it, depending on what the level of demand is year round in your locality.

You will find that most of your potential tenants are a savvy bunch who will be viewing several properties before finding what they believe is the best deal.

Another point to consider is the small print on your mortgage. Most buy to let lenders will want you to cover at least 125% of your mortgage payments with your rental income. You will need to be certain you can cover this with the rent you are charging.

Managing Property Yourself vs Using A Letting Agent

You may be at the point where you are considering allowing your letting agent to handle more than just the advertising of your property. A lot will depend on how much time you have to self-manage and whether you will even want to handle various issues with your tenants.

The thought of the latter can make some people bury their head in their hands. It can be difficult handling all the paperwork and various deadlines and if you happen to be having a stressful time in your day job, self-managing your tenants will almost certainly result in added hassle if not now but sooner or later.

One thing you can count on with self-managing, is the savings you can make on estate agent fees. These can really add up over time and if the money you save outweighs the stresses then you won't necessarily need an estate agent at all.

Of course the big advantage of using an estate agent to begin with is being able to advertise your property on property portals such as Rightmove and Zoopla. To advertise on these platforms is expensive unless you have a large volume of properties, therefore the only way to get your property listed is to go through an estate agent on the high street or use an online estate agent.

Increasingly nowadays, other forms of advertising your property are springing up to break the stranglehold of estate agents. In fact the traditional estate agent is threatened by the rise of online estate agents, social media and websites such as Gumtree which either charge small fees or nothing at all to advertise your property.

That said, there is more to being an estate agent than simply being a window to advertise property. A good estate agent will not only ensure that all your paperwork is in order, they will also help you with various issues that may confront you as a landlord.

This includes advising and giving you notice of changes in laws, handling tenant deposits and dealing with any issue that may arise if you have the misfortune of having to deal with a bad tenant. Not everyone is cut out to be a landlord and handle these sorts of problems.

Of course you might also find that you have absolutely nothing to deal with during a tenancy in which case you will be saving what amounts to a hefty monthly fee for doing next to nothing.

To help you decide if getting a lettings agent to manage your property is right for you here are the services offered by a typical estate agent.

Let only

Under a let only arrangement, your letting agent will handle a lot of the initial administration including the handling of tenant deposits, signing of tenancy agreements, credit checks, property viewings and so on.

Managed

If you instruct a letting agent to manage the property for you, they will look after all the day-to-day management of the property in return for proportion of the rent you make each month. This can vary a lot between agents with the average being 10% plus VAT.

Their duties will include collecting rents each month, dealing with any tenant issues on your behalf, organising property repairs, safety inspections and so on. Sometimes a new piece of legislation might come in such as Rent Smart Wales, which require either an investment in training or extra costs. In cases where landlords need to jump through various hoops to be able to let their properties, simply letting a qualified estate agent handle it can save you time and effort.

Landlords who own multiple properties are more likely to find this option attractive due to the time saving factor. If you are just starting out as a property developer, you will need to weigh up if going for a managed option is worthwhile considering the extra cost.

Potential pitfalls of advertising lettings yourself

If you have decided to go it alone and manage your investment property yourself, then you might also be considering ways to save even more money and take the letting agent out of the equation altogether.

Before you do this, however, there are as ever some pros and cons to advertising property yourself rather than use a letting agent to do the work for you.

First of all though let's look at the positives.

The first thing you will save of course is your money. You can advertise a property on Gumtree for free even if the likely traffic you will get for a free advert is lower than you will get from dedicated property portals Rightmove and Zoopla.

You will also need to take your own photographs, write your own description of the property and organise an energy performance certificate to fulfil your legal obligations when it comes to advertising a property.

You will then need to ensure that your description is accurate. There is no point in exaggerating or underselling your property if you are trying to attract tenants.

One of the biggest drawbacks with going it alone is not having access to the big two property portals. Fortunately there are ways to get around this by using online estate agents who will charge you a lot less to have your property listed than your local estate agent.

Now for some of the negatives of going it alone...

Going it alone will certainly result in you having to work harder to find a good tenant. One problem with using free advertising is its potential to attract the wrong kind of tenants.

If you are not going through your estate agent, it will be up to you to investigate the suitability of potential tenants a process which is fraught with danger. The kind of tenants you don't want living in your property are just the ones who are looking for landlords who self-manage and advertise their properties on Gumtree and so on.

If you do think the risk is worth it, then prepare yourself for being messed around by some people who are either unable to provide a reference or reluctant to provide evidence of their identity.

Using an online estate agent vs traditional estate agent

Selling your property used to be a matter of calling up your estate agent and allowing them to do the rest. Today things are a lot more complicated.

The Internet has revolutionised our shopping habits and we are seeing this play out with every closure of a major high street chain. Traditional estate agents are also now at risk of becoming victims of this revolution which is bad news for them and, temporarily at least, good news for you if you are aiming to sell a property because you now get to choose from different fee structures.

Of course at the root of this revolution was the arrival of Rightmove and Zoopla. These are the two most dominant portals when it comes to online searches for property and the websites where your property is most likely to be found.

Both traditional and online estate agents will advertise your properties on these portals for a fee, which can vary considerably depending on which option you choose. That choice will depend on a range of considerations you will need to look at before choosing which option to go for.

The main points to consider are fees, viewings, customer service and local knowledge.

Fees

Fees are potentially the most important consideration when it comes to selling your property. Bricks and mortar estate agents will charge between 1% and 3% of the property value.

Compare this to an online estate agent which can cost as little as £30 a month for a no frills service and the savings can be significant, assuming of course you can sell your property fast without any of the extras that go with a traditional estate agent's service.

One of the advantages of using a traditional estate agent to sell your house is that you won't need to pay them anything until after the property is sold.

Viewings

Depending on the level of demand in your chosen location, you may have several viewings to arrange and if you are using a traditional estate agent, they will handle all this for you. This is particularly useful if you don't have the time to accompany viewings yourself.

If you use an online estate agent, you will probably be arranging and attending viewings yourself, which will take up more of your time. If you don't feel comfortable doing viewings yourself and feel that an estate agent will have better negotiating skills, then it might be better in this case to use a traditional estate agent. Being able to negotiate the right price is key to selling your property and making a profit you can use to go on and develop more properties.

Customer Service

One thing you are unlikely to get from an online estate agent is dedicated customer service, beyond a telephone call. Agents working for online estate agents will be dealing with high volumes of calls every day making it impossible to give each client more than a few minutes of time.

You may not get great customer service with a traditional estate agent either but at least you will be able to put a face to a name.

Local knowledge

If you are looking at local knowledge then here again a traditional estate agent will have the edge over using an online agent. A bricks and mortar estate agent will have years of experience in a particular area, however with records of house prices and rents now freely available online, it is questionable whether local knowledge will be important in the ultimate goal of selling your property.

Ultimately much will depend on your own individual circumstances and your decision shouldn't necessarily rest on fees. Any savings could be cancelled out if you can't negotiate a good price and those low monthly fees could start to add up in any case if your property remains unsold.

The importance of a good landlord/tenant relationship

If getting the right tenant to sign up to live in your property was the hard part, then becoming a landlord for the first time will also offer up its own unique set of challenges. These challenges are likely to be fewer if you are able to maintain a good landlord/tenant relationship from the start.

The first step to a good client tenant relationship is understanding each other. While your first aim is to be paid your rent very month on time, your tenant's desires will rest on being provided with a safe place to live left free from intrusion.

While safety is a primary concern, maintaining the right balance between not intruding on your tenant's enjoyment of the property and paying enough attention to show that you care is tricky.

There are no guarantees that following these rules will mean you and your tenant live happily ever after but here's what you can do to make sure there is less chance of the relationship turning sour.

Keep your promises

The fastest way to annoy most people is to break your promises. If an appliance has gone wrong and you have promised to replace it, then do so as soon as you can. The longer it takes, the more room there is for your tenant to start thinking you're not bothered.

Make regular checks

While it's easy to slip into a comfort zone as a landlord, it is important to inspect your property regularly if only to keep an eye on what your tenant is getting up to. While most people are trustworthy, a lot can happen to a property as the months fly by. Your tenant is not going to mind these checks if you tell them it is simply to make sure everything is working as it should.

Be available in case of emergencies

Your tenant will appreciate being able to contact you, if their boiler bursts or there is some other emergency situation. They won't like it if you are unavailable or out of the country in their hour of need and there is no backup.

It has to be considered that becoming a landlord means accepting certain responsibilities. These responsibilities will grow as you expand your portfolio.

10 Mistakes New Landlords Should Avoid At All Costs!

1. Not checking tenant references and their credit history

If your number one aim is to make money from your investment in property, then starting out with a bad tenant who doesn't pay their rent can be a huge drain on your funds. This is less likely to happen if you make it a priority to check their credit rating and get hold of a reliable reference. You simply cannot afford to take people at face value.

2. Not checking passports

New rules mean you could be fined heavily for providing accommodation for illegal immigrants. Check the government's latest advice on how to determine if a tenant has a right to rent in the UK.

3. Imagining that voids are only happen to other landlords

No matter what your tenant says at the beginning of the tenancy, most will probably move on in two or three years, therefore you need to be prepared to act quickly when you receive notice your tenant wants to move out.

4. Not putting aside funds for repairs

Maintaining a property can be an expensive business. Older properties, houses in particular will require the most ongoing maintenance, therefore be prepared for some big bills. Wear and tear will also become an issue over time and replacing fitted kitchens can make a hole of several thousand pounds. Unfortunately, you will have no choice other than to keep your property in good working order, or face the prospect of lengthy voids.

5. Failing to comply with local authority rules for landlords

The government makes regular attempts to change the rules when it comes to buy to let. Many of these rules are designed to make life easier for tenants rather than landlords. Ignore them and you could leave yourself open to fines.

6. Not sticking to the terms of the tenancy agreement

If say you stipulate in the agreement that there are no pets, then allowing your tenant to keep a pet 'just this once' will invalidate the agreement in this respect and leave you open to further abuses of the terms in the contract between you and the tenant.

7. Failing to act decisively when rental payments are missed

If your tenant has stopped paying the rent act quickly to make sure they pay up. One month can soon turn into two months and if you need to evict your tenant then that will only add a few more months before your property starts earning you money again.

8. Not carrying out safety checks

It is vital you arrange for gas safety checks and make sure the property you are letting is safe to live in. Failing to do this will leave you at the mercy of a judge and with your name in the newspapers if something catastrophic happens.

9. Treating buy to let as a hobby

Developing property for profit might sound fun but if you have been reading this book you will understand that it is a serious business and it needs to be treated like one.

10. Not renewing tenancy agreements

If you want to reduce voids it is always better to try to hang on to a good tenant rather than search for a new one. Standard tenancy agreements last for 6 months after which they revert to a rolling contract. This means the tenant only has to give you a month's notice to leave.

Finding a new tenant could potentially take months to achieve so getting your tenant to sign up for another 6 months will at least remove the nagging worries that they could leave at any time.

PART FIVE:

Building A Portfolio

Chapter 10

The Next Steps

Congratulations! No doubt you will now be the owner of your first development property. Now you will be thinking, what next? How do I go from investing in developing my first property to someone who owns a portfolio of 50 or more properties?

You may be surprised to hear that the vast majority of buy to let landlords out there stop at just one or two properties even though they will be reaping the benefits of those initial investments for years to come.

This is a bit of a mystery considering that their returns will only have multiplied if they had built up a portfolio.

So why do most property investors draw the line at less than a handful of properties?

Because they think only in terms of the income they receive from sources other than the properties they have invested in.

So, for example their monthly income might be £3,000 per month and the mortgages on each of their properties will be say £500 multiply this by two and this doesn't leave a lot of money left to pay life's other expenses.

All of us only have so much disposable income and you may be surprised how many successful investors started out on below average salaries even if everyone assumes they were that wealthy to begin with.

As you get more involved in the next level of property investment, you begin to find out what their secret is.

Well if you have been paying attention in this book, you will realise that everything starts with that first investment. Choosing the right property that will provide the firm foundation is the key to all your future success.

As any property developer will tell you, the first property is always the hardest because that is usually the one you are investing in with your disposable income.

Your goal in property investment is to use less and less of that disposable income and use the properties themselves to generate the income you need to expand your portfolio.

To do this you will need to start with a steady flow of cash from your tenants who will essentially be paying your mortgage. This is only one part of the equation. The second will be that magic ingredient we call equity.

If rental income is the fuel that maintains your portfolio, the equity you have in your property is the part you can use to really begin to expand your portfolio. The more equity you have in each of your properties the more money you can raise to fund further development projects.

Generating finance to expand your portfolio

So how can you release all that equity tied up in your first buy to let property? You can do this in two ways.

You could sell the property. Assuming that your property has risen in equity terms over 12 months plus the money you put into it as a deposit, you can then use that money as a deposit on your next property.

In a perfect world, you could go on doing this but as has become painfully apparent in recent years, you can't rely on property price growth alone. In any case if you sell the property, you then wave goodbye to the extra income you could make through letting it.

This leaves us with the second option.

You can borrow against the equity to fund another house purchase. This means you will maintain the momentum you need to build a portfolio quickly. Why take the long route saving for deposits with your disposable income, when you can simply borrow against the equity you already have tied up in your first buy to let property?

Of course, you will still need to be careful not to over commit yourself on mortgage payments. Assuming you have done your homework, there is less risk if those payments are covered through the income you make from letting your property.

Interest Only Mortgages

One of the advantages of using interest only loans to fund the expansion of your buy to let portfolio are the lower repayments. With a typical mortgage, you will be paying back the full value of the property over time which means monthly payments are a lot higher.

An interest only mortgage can be the best option for if you are an investor who wants to minimise monthly repayments and who expect to sell off their portfolio. As I am not a financial advisor I cannot say categorically that this will work for you but it is and option that is well worth considering. Always have a good accountant and mortgage broker in your power team.

Making a business out of property development

You will notice that one of the central themes running through this book is treating property development as a business. To have any chance of expanding your portfolio you will need a good level of business sense.

Most people fail at buy to let for the same reasons people fail at business – they don't have positive cash flow. Cashflow is everything to a business as it is to property development.

The properties you invest in should be paying you to invest in them rather than the other way around. This way you will have more than enough to pay mortgages, expenses and anything else that might come your way on a rainy day.

By continuing to purchase cashflowing property, you will be multiplying your income to the point where you won't need to turn up for work anymore. Your goal is to reach the point where your income is passive which means you are making money whether you choose to work or not.

Maintaining your portfolio

Like any business, there will be ongoing costs associated with property development. I'm not going to pretend that all the money you make is pure profit.

IF you are a property developer, the houses you invest in will need ongoing investment not only to keep them in good order, but also to increase their value over time.

By doing even the most minor work such as giving your properties a fresh coat of paint, you will be increasing the level of rent and capital growth over time. By carefully increasing the value of your properties over time, you will find raising money for deposits on additional properties much easier.

Summary

I hope you have found this a useful introduction to starting out as a property developer.

My aim with this book was to cover the basics of investment for beginners and to pass on the knowledge I have gained in the past two decades as a property investor.

In that time, I have expanded my portfolio to more than 200 properties and after experiencing the freedom that it gives me to spend time with my family and travel the world, I wanted to share that knowledge so that you can one day do the same.

As one wise person once said to me the more you learn about investing the less money you need to make a lot of money. Don't just use this book to learn about property investment, seek out books written by other experts in the field, attend seminars and speak to other investors about their experiences.

Without this education, you will find it a much harder road to financial freedom or that road will be so long you will never get the chance to enjoy the fruits of your endeavours.

An investment in knowledge pays the best interest

Benjamin Franklin

Even more...
...from Nick Fox Property Mentoring.

Thank you for taking the time to read our book; we hope you've found it helpful. If you'd like to extend your knowledge, please check out our website, where you'll find a wealth of free information and details of our mentoring packages.

We offer a range of mentoring options to suit all needs, from short intensive taster sessions to more comprehensive packages that will give you a deeper understanding of property investment and the buy to let market, focusing on the rewards and implications of building an HMO portfolio.

Various choices available include:
- Half-day 'HMO Education and Tour'
- One-day 'Intensive HMO Property Mentoring Course'
- Two-day 'Intensive HMO Property Mentoring Course'
- 12 months' full access to and support from Nick Fox and his Power Team

Whichever package you choose, you can be assured that Nick's commitment to your personal property goals are absolute. Nick and his team get a real kick out of watching others grow their property portfolios by helping them implement the most successful methods that have been tried and tested over many years.

As skilled and experienced professionals, we present our mentoring sessions in such a way that they are easy to understand, while enabling highly effective learning. The acute insights and practical methodology on offer will help you to take your property business to the next level and secure financial independence for you and your loved ones.

Check out our website **www.nickfox.co.uk** or call us on **01908 930369** to find out more.

Find us on FACEBOOK Nick Fox Mentor TWITTER @foxytowers
www.nickfox.co.uk EMAIL hello@nickfox.co.uk TEL 01908 930369
NICK FOX PROPERTY MENTORING
14 Wharfside Bletchley Milton Keynes MK2 2AZ

Read on...

Collect the set of books by Nick Fox to help you achieve financial freedom through property investment.

HMO PROPERTY SUCCESS

Do you want a secure financial future that starts sooner, rather than later as you're approaching retirement? By investing in multi-let properties, you can double or even triple the level of rental income generated by single letting, and realise positive cash flow from the start. In this book, multiple business owner and investor, Nick Fox, clearly guides you through the steps to building an HMO portfolio that delivers both on-going income and a tangible pension or lifestyle pot.

ISBN: 978-0-9576516-0-9
RRP: £9.99

PROPERTY INVESTMENT SUCCESS

How does your financial future look?
If you haven't reviewed your pension provision for a while or aren't completely happy with how your current investments are performing, you should take a closer look at property. In this book, Nick Fox discusses the pros and cons of traditional pensions and makes the case for property as a robust alternative investment vehicle.
He looks at how property can deliver different kinds of returns at different times and shows how you can build a tailored portfolio that perfectly satisfies your own future financial needs.

ISBN: 978-0-9576516-4-7
RRP: £9.99

THE SECRETS OF BUY TO LET SUCCESS

Are you looking for a sound investment that can give you both income and growth on your capital, but nervous about the future of the property market? This book will put your mind at rest. In The Secrets of Buy to Let Success, Nick Fox shares his knowledge and expertise about the market, guiding the reader step by step through the basics of building a solid and profitable property business - even through an economic crisis. If you're completely new to property investment, this book is a great place to start.

ISBN: 978-0-9927817-2-9
RRP: £9.99

101 TOP TIPS FOR PROPERT INVESTMENT SUCCESS

Whether you're looking to focus purely on HMOs, build a varied portfolio of rental properties, or employ a number of different strategies to make money from property, '101 TOP TIPS' is full of useful information that will help keep you at the top of the property investment business.
Nick Fox has spent the past decade amassing a highly profitable buy to let portfolio and continues to invest in a variety of property projects and business ventures. His tailored mentoring programmes have helped many aspiring investors realise their own potential in the property field.

ISBN: 978-0-9935074-9-6 | RRP: £9.99

PROPERTY RENNOVATION & REFURBISHMENT SUCCESS

Successful renovation and refurbishment relies on spending the right amount of money in the right way, so are you ready to hone your budgeting, planning and project-management skills? Alongside the deposit, this is where the biggest chunk of your investment funds will be spent. You need to analyse the figures, budget correctly, plan the work in detail and ensure it's carried out properly so that your buy to let performs as you need it to. Not sure how to do that? Then this is the book for you!

ISBN: 978-0-9927817-6-7
RRP: £11.99

COMPLETE PROPERTY INVESTMENT SUCCESS

This indispensable trilogy takes you through the pros and cons of property as an investment vehicle, looks at the business of buy to let and the different ways you can make money from property, then goes into detail about how to successfully source, refurbish and let out highly cash-positive houses in multiple occupation.

ISBN: 978-0-9927817-0-5
RRP: £26.99

COMPLETE HMO PROPERTY SUCCESS

This HMO 'superbook' is essential reading for anyone who's starting out in property investment and wants to generate income.

It begins by looking at investing in Houses in Multiple Occupation as a business and takes you through how to successfully source, refurbish, let out and manage a highly cash-positive portfolio.

The second part then focuses on the all-important renovation stage. It details how to budget, plan your works, manage your project and carry out the refurbishment in such a way that your HMO performs as you need it to and you get the returns you're looking for.

A prolific and highly successful investor, Nick's personal portfolio extends to more than 200 properties, both shared accommodation and single household lets – and he also has interests in several development projects around the UK.

ISBN: 978-0-9935074-0-3 | RRP: £19.99

Available now online at
www.amazon.co.uk & www.nickfox.co.uk
Books, iBook, Kindle & Audio

Find us on FACEBOOK Nick Fox Mentor TWITTER NickFoxPropertyMentoring
www.nickfox.co.uk EMAIL hello@nickfox.co.uk TEL 01908 930369
NICK FOX PROPERTY MENTORING
14 Wharfside Bletchley Milton Keynes MK2 2AZ

Write a review and get free stuff!

If you've enjoyed what you've read, why not tell other people and bag yourself some free stuff in the process?

Simply write a review of this compilation — or any of the other books in the 'SUCCESS' series and publicise it via:

- Amazon
- iTunes
- Facebook
- Twitter
- Your blog

... or any other online or offline publications.

Then email an image or link to us at hello@nickfox.co.uk.

We'll thank you via Twitter and you'll get back some exclusive property investment tools and samples of our latest materials to help you stay focused and up to date in your investment journey.

Thanks in advance and we hope to hear from you soon!

Testimonials

This is just some of the positive feedback I've received from happy mentoring clients over the past few years:

"I met Nick a number of years ago and was immediately struck by his deep knowledge and experience in the field of property investing. No problem is ever too great a challenge for Nick - his creative entrepreneur spirit is a joy to behold. He is both dynamic and detailed, great fun to work with and quite truly inspirational. He is now my business partner and good friend."
Richard Leonard

"Nick and his team are the real deal. Their knowledge and help in moving my investment project forward has been invaluable. Without their expertise I would not have been able to reach my personal property goals or milestones."
Richard Felton, UK

"Great book, great guy and great results for me after I read 'HMO Property Success'. I've now replaced my job with passive income from HMO properties. Thanks, Nick!"
C.Clark, Bedford

"Nick is a very experienced property professional. His practical advice on setting goals, the pros and cons of this type of investment

and how to minimise risks and properly manage a growing portfolio are essential in what can be a very complex investment. Nick's mentoring is not a get-rich-quick formula but a clear and concise way of demonstrating how a solid property investment strategy can be put into action. And the results are well worth it."

D. Wright, Aberdeen

"I have spent money in the past on various property courses, where you are taught in a group in a classroom, and those have not really helped me. This one-to-one mentoring with Nick was brilliant, as I was actually seeing his business and properties, meeting tenants, getting lots of advice and seeing what worked well and what didn't in a live situation. I have booked another two days with Nick in my home city next week, to look at various properties and hopefully start my journey as a full-time property investor, and I cannot wait! I highly recommend this type of mentoring!"

James Robinson, Hull

"Both Sarah and I cannot express how much help Nick has been to our property business over the last two years. His support and knowledge have been invaluable. We would thoroughly recommend his mentoring to any budding investor."

Stuart Lewis, Northampton

"Thank you so much for your patience, professionalism and general understanding during our three-day mentoring programme. The visit to see how your office and HMO business runs was incredible and so, so helpful. Without it we would have been at a complete loss. With your guidance and help we

have now purchased our first HMO property and look forward to keeping in touch to show you our profitable progress!"
Rebecca Santay-Jones, Harrow

"I first met Nick in the autumn of 2012 when I was looking for someone to guide me through my first HMO purchase. Nick's mentoring was invaluable and gave me such a good grounding - not just in HMOs, but in how to run a successful property business - that I have been able to move forward with real confidence as my business has grown. Even now, if there is something I am uncertain of, or I just want to bounce an idea around, I'm very grateful to have Nick in my corner. He has such wide-ranging experience in the industry and I value his opinion greatly. The income my portfolio already provides gives me the option of going part-time in my day job and in the coming months, as I grow the business further, I fully intend to become a full-time property investor and landlord."
Andy Potter, Fareham

"Today's experience has been brilliant – it really opened up my eyes up to the world of HMOs and made me see properties in a different light, in terms of understanding just how much potential each one has. Your experience has accelerated my learning and shown me how important it is to have the right mindset when getting into this area of property investing.

As a kinaesthetic learner, I really enjoyed the hands-on experience of going from property to property and getting a flavour of how you see and do things. Your openness and honesty is what I appreciated the most and has reaffirmed to me that I have made

the right choice. Looking forward to getting that first property!"
Gabriel F, Enfield

"Nick has clearly got a huge amount of knowledge in his field, and having his support and experience has given me the increased confidence to make my first steps into investing."
Craig Smith, Edinburgh

0330 — 124 2392

Lightning Source UK Ltd.
Milton Keynes UK
UKHW02f070707061 8
323877UK00011B/1514/P